The *Write* words

The Write Words
poetry, quotes,
crafty sayings,
& scriptures
for all of life's topics

selected by
Crystal Dawn Perry

ClearSky Publishing
Hixson, Tennessee

The Write Words

A very special thanks to all of the contributors for making this book an incredible compilation. Every effort has been made to give proper credit for each poem and quote. In the event of any question, we regret the error and will be glad to give proper credit in future editions of this book. The bible scriptures are from several sources including, but not limited to, the New International Version and the New King James Version.

The Write Words
ClearSky Publishing
P.O. Box 606-B Hixson, TN. 37343

Printed in the United States of America

Library of Congress Control Number 2002115024
1st ed.
Hixson, TN : ClearSky Pub., 2003
p. cm.

ISBN 0-9706381-1-6

I dedicate this book to all of the poetic, quotable, and brilliant minds that have contributed to this book and to the ones that are crafty enough to use these verses to create a beautiful treasure; also to my babysitters - Brittany, and grandmothers, Pat and Sandy, whom are among the brilliant, crafty minds.

A powerful agent is the right word.

–Mark Twain

A few suggestions for getting the most out of

The Write Words:

❖ Use the cross-references. Cross-references are used when the verses for another topic are suitable but are too numerous to repeat the entire list under both headings. Ex. –When looking for a quote for "Scrapbooks", you will be cross-referenced to "Memories." If you do not consider these verses too, you may miss out on the perfect words that you were hoping to express.

❖ Don't be afraid to change or omit a word, or even an entire line, to suit your needs. These poems and verses are for your personal use – personalize them!

❖ Many uplifting and thoughtful verses are listed under "Life" that can be used for most general purposes.

❖ The blank lines found after the "Poetry" and "Quotes, Crafty sayings, and Scriptures" sections should be used to jot down inspired craft ideas or additional verses.

❖ In the "Quotes, Crafty sayings, and Scriptures" section, you will find sayings listed first under each topic, then all quotes, and then scriptures, if available.

Poetry
Table of Contents
for all of life's topics

Quotes, Sayings, and Scriptures
Table of Contents
for all of life's topics

A child is the greatest poem ever known.

-Christopher Morley

Poetry

Adoption
I've waited so long
To have you to hold
But now I clearly see
God was making arrangements
For you to be with me.

-Crystal Dawn Perry

Air Force
(see also Military)
The power in flight
The power to be
Soaring to heights
That most people never see

Discipline and training
Dedication every day
Thank you, men and women
Of our Air Force, U.S.A.

-Gina Marie Lauchner

Amusement Park
A Land of Imagination
Is waiting just for me
I can't wait to get there
All the great things I will see
"We're almost there", Daddy says
It's just beyond the trees
We're here, we're here, we're really here!
How much fun it's going to be!

-Dana Roberts Clark

Freedom is my greatest asset.
Fear is something I haven't met.

-Shelley Howington

14

Angel

To your guardian Angel,
I have to say,
"Please watch out
for my baby today!"
-Shelley Howington

Darling little one,
With eyes like mine
And tiny little hands
On day to capture the world,
My Angel Child
Sweet Angel Child
You are my gift from God.
-Najah T. Clemmons

You have the face of an angel
With your beautiful smile
No one can resist those eyes—
What undeniable style!
-Linda Price
Little Lace Lady, Chattanooga Choo-Choo

Anniversary

Happy Yesterdays, Happier Tomorrows
Even when life brings us sorrow
With God as my captain and I as your wife
I could not have asked for a better life.
-Dana Roberts Clark

I don't always show it
But look in my heart and you will see
How much I really love you
Happy Anniversary!
-Dana Roberts Clark

I loved you then, I love you now
But time has changed me somehow
The wild and reckless love I felt
The way you made my heart melt
Has slipped away through the years
We've both cried many tears
But the love I feel for you today
Is a better love in every way
Because I know you will be by my side
In your heart I can confide
I love you now, I loved you then
Thank you for being my best friend
-Dana Roberts Clark

The older you get the more you hold on
But before you know it, the day is gone.
Cherish each smile, each laugh, and each tear.
You blink your eyes and one day becomes a year.
-Dana Roberts Clark

Forever you did pledge to each other and
now half of a century has passed.
Incredibly you've walked through the trials of life, with
still an amazing friendship that lasts.
Faithfully you have nourished one another,
despite the obstacles that have been at your door.
Triumphantly you stand together,
with a love stronger than ever before.
Years of laughter, moments of tears and
half a century of joy.
May God bless you with **FIFTY** more.

Happy Anniversary.
-Lisa M. Billings

Marriage is more than just the word love.
It is trust, honesty, and friendship-
gifts sent from Heaven above.

-Dana Roberts Clark

Army
(see also Military)

Over the mountains and through the woods,
The Army is on the go.
They will stand and fight till the very end,
To protect us from our foes.

-Dana Roberts Clark

Attitude

Did you see my little foot
Stomping on the ground?
Come on momma, I'm ready...
Let's go another round.

-Dana Roberts Clark

Baby
(see also Boy, Child, Daughter, Girl, Son and Toddler)

10 perfect fingers and
10 perfect toes
Mommy's eyes and
Daddy's nose
A wonderful miracle
From heaven above
Oh, little baby,
How much you are loved!

-Dana Roberts Clark

Welcome to the world-
It's going to be quite a show.
First, there's something important
I want you to always know:
You are my shining moon; you are my glistening sun.
You are my inner peace; you are my abundant fun.
You are my roaming land; you are my wavy sea,
You are, and always will be, everything to me.

-Crystal Dawn Perry

Darling little one,
With eyes like mine
And tiny little hands
On day to capture the world,
My Angel Child
Sweet Angel Child
You are my gift from God.

-Najah T. Clemmons

The love of a child makes you change
And become all that they will aspire to.
The blessing of a child makes you appreciate life
And hold on to those little hands
That God has given to you.

-Lisa M. Billings

Tiny hands and tiny feet
And those bright blue eyes
Innocence shines from you abound
Truly you are from heaven's skies.

-Suzanne Smith

Have you ever heard an angle breath
The soft whisper of a sound?
Have you felt her breath upon your cheek
And watched her chest fall up and down?
Have you glanced into that perfect face
And thought what a beautiful girl
And realized how much God has blessed you?
"I Love You more than this whole world."

-Dana Roberts Clark

A little game of peek-a-boo
Is baby's way to play
It's so much fun to peak and hide
We do it everyday!

-Linda Price
Little Lace Lady, Chattanooga Choo-Choo

I didn't know what to expect
The first time I saw your face
But I fell in love with you instantly.
No one will ever take your place.

-Dana Roberts Clark

Ball

Basketballs, baseballs, any kind of ball,
Just throw me one and I'll have fun.
Big balls, little balls any ball at all,
If I'm playing ball, my smiles have just begun.
Light ones, bright ones, I'll catch them all.
I think I may go pro; Let me show you how it's done.

-Crystal Dawn Perry

Baptism

Wonderful people, who for you will pray
Asking God to save your soul today
Your burdens at the cross you can lay

Only Jesus can save your soul
For the asking, you life he can control

To him, if you will cling
Heaven's gates your soul will sing
Evermore with Jesus, your cares to bring

Christ is the way, truth, life and light
Right now is the time with Jesus to unite
Only God knows if you'll have another night
Salvation, God's plan on your soul he'll write
Since at the altar you made it right

-Shelley Howington

Baseball

Watch the ball all the way in.
Swing the bat level with your chin.
Now run as fast as you can.
Listen to the roar of the baseball fans!

-Dana Roberts Clark

Bath

The bubbles dance and tickle your nose
When bath time comes each day.
We wash your hair and scrub your toes
As you laugh and splash and play!

-Linda Price
Little Lace Lady, Chattanooga Choo-Choo

An empty bathtub, cold and white,
Transforms when you come near.
It rejoices at the sight,
Of a little one so dear.

The coldness goes away,
With one flash of your smile.
Its bubbling water seems to say,
"Will you stay a while?"

You hide behind its curtain,
Playing peek-a-boo,
But you're never really certain,
Whether I'll find you.

The rubber ducky swims along,
Not knowing what else to do,
And then you sing your favorite song,
And ducky starts singing too!

You splash the water to and fro,
And then you start to yawn,
This bath time play is really fun,
But you woke up at dawn!

The warming water is replaced,
By my warm arms instead.
You wrap your legs around my waist,
And I carry you off to bed.

-Aparna Iyer

Frothy beards made with soapy bubbles
are such a comical sight
And looking in the mirror is needed
to make sure that it's just right.
Rubber duckies, fun-shaped sponges,
toy boats ready to set sail.
Squirt guns, splashing, sudsy soap
and many a bath time tale.
Soon wrinkled fingers and toes will be
begging for another minute.
And when they're done we long to be
relaxing and soaking in it!

-Laura Taylor Mark

Beach

You are my shining moon; you are my glistening sun.
You are my inner peace; you are my abundant fun.
You are my roaming land; you are my wavy sea,
You are, and always will be, everything to me.

-Crystal Dawn Perry

Seagull cries and crashing waves,
The echo of a large conch shell,
The warmth of sand between my toes
A pool of silk within my pail.
Some surf, some sun, some water.
A place to touch the sea
And share a moment of my life
With you along the beach.

-R. Dee Waltz-Daniels

Sand, Water, Splish, Splash
"Hey! Look at this!"
Play, Run, Splish, Splash
What an active little fish!

-Crystal Dawn Perry

Birthday

The older you get the more you hold on
But before you know it the day is gone.
Cherish each smile, each laugh, and each tear.
You blink your eyes and one day becomes a year.

-Dana Roberts Clark

It's time for a cake
Some candles
Hooray!
Today is my 3rd birthday.

-Dana Roberts Clark

Happy Birthday, little girl.
You're growing up so fast.
I wish these moments of our lives
Did not so quickly pass.

-Linda Price
Little Lace Lady, Chattanooga Choo-Choo

Another inch taller
Another shoe size too small
Another grade that passes
New supplies for new classes
Another book that is read
New words to comprehend
Another birthday gift opened
Another day I am hoping
Another tear in my eye
Will slow these years going by.

-Gina Marie Lauchner

Fifteen years ago you were only three,
growing more and more curious of the world around
you each day. You were my precious baby boy and the
thought of you some day becoming a young man was
so far away.

Ten years ago you were only eight,
growing more independent, becoming more perceptive
of the world around you each day. A baby boy you
were no more. Still, the thought of you graduating
high school; making decisions without me, was
something too far down the road to look for.

Five years ago you were thirteen,
growing more precocious, with such self-awareness
that would sometimes leave me speechless.
I knew that my baby boy was growing up,
but part of me was not ready nonetheless.

Today you are eighteen,
and this is just the beginning for you.
I cannot hold your hand anymore
to keep you safe while crossing the street.
I cannot tell you not to tell you whom you should trust
and not trust out of the many you will meet.

Because today you are eighteen,
when just the other day you were three.
Once my baby boy and now my young man, I thank
God for all of those years and the blessing of you that
he has given me.

Happy Birthday
-Lisa M. Billings

Boxing
Sometimes you hit 'em high.
Sometimes you hit' em low
But keep your feet on the go.
Punch with the left.
Punch with the right.
Always keep their chin in your sight.
Whatever you do
Don't let the fight end
With the referee
Counting you to ten.

-Dana Roberts Clark

Boy/Boys
A cape to hide your secret powers
Swords can make you smile for hours
Magic spells and wizard's wand
In far off lands you greet the dawn.

-Julie Perkins Cantrell

He's a little touch of heaven
Sent down from above.
He's filled our lives with happiness
And our hearts full of love.

-Dana Roberts Clark

Rough and tumble, climbing trees,
Cuts, scrapes, bandaged skinned knees.

Dump trucks, fire engines, shiny red cars,
Bugs, worms, grass and dirt in a jar.

Mischievous twinkle in their bright eyes,
Little all stars and one of the guys!

-Laura Taylor Mark

Boy Scouts
Sharing one day, once a week
With other boys to knowledge seek.
Receiving badges for a talent learned
A wonderful remembrance, you strive to earn.
Lending boys an opportunity
And giving much to the community.
                    -Brenda Darlene Kijowski

Break-up
Now you are gone and I'm all alone
For you there is someone new
But tell me something,
Does her smile melt your heart
The way mine used to do?
                    -Dana Roberts Clark

Brother
I've been blessed to have
A brother like you.
You're my pal, my buddy,
And my best friend too.
                    -Dana Roberts Clark

It means a lot to me
Having a brother like you
I don't say it often enough
But believe me it is true
You put other people first
And I'd like to suggest
That of all the brothers in the world
You surely are the best!
                    -John Beith

Precious brother can you see
What the Lord has given you and me?
The chance to grow and find our way;
But, still we cannot stay away.

Not just a name upon a tree.
The Lord has made us family.
To share our lives both good and bad,
To come together happy or sad.

A helping hand within our grasp,
A friendship that you know will last.
Not just a name upon a tree;
The Lord has made us family.

Thankful I shall always be,
The Lord has made you brother to me.

-Brenda Darlene Kijowski

The bond of brothers stands the test of time.
I'm so blessed that you are mine.

-Dana Roberts Clark

Butterfly

My heart, I'll send to thee.
Wisps of color in the air;
Butterflies from me.

They travel on a gentle breeze
To wherever you may be
Painting hearts with kisses,
Just as those you've sent to me.

-Brenda Darlene Kijowski

Camping

Sticks and sleeping bags and ants
Dirty hands and grass-stained pants
Gathering wood and piling up leaves
Carrying toilet paper and finding a tree
Sitting by a fire and dodging the sparks
There's nothing greater than
The great outdoors after dark.

-Gina Marie Lauchner

Cat

My kitty is so special.
She's such a loving pet.
She knows when I am happy
And she knows when I'm upset.

-Linda Price
Little Lace Lady, Chattanooga Choo-Choo

A pair of warm hands cups him
And lifts him to the sky
Kitty finds he's looking
Into a pair of loving eyes.

-Brenda Darlene Kijowski

Sometimes you're almost human.

You're a "fur"st rate pet.

I'm "feline" like there's a "purrr"son
waiting to be "whisker"ed away
under those cat eyes.

You're "meow"tstanding.

-Gina Marie Lauchner

Child/Children

(see also Baby, Boy, Daughter, Girl, Son, Teenager & Toddler)

Tiny hands and tiny feet
And those bright blue eyes
Innocence shines from you abound
Truly you are from heaven's skies.

-Suzanne Smith

The older they get the more you hold on
But before you know it the day is gone.
Cherish each smile, each laugh, and each tear.
You blink your eyes and one day becomes a year.

-Dana Roberts Clark

After school it's time to play;
We all have fun in different ways.
You might be a boxer or play ball
Or paint pretty pictures on your walls.
You might sing or dance or play in a band.
However you spend your time,
I'm your biggest fan.

-Dana Roberts Clark

Cute as a button I've always heard
But I've always thought they were just words
Because there's no way a button could be
As cute as you are to me.

-Dana Roberts Clark

She's a little touch of heaven
Sent down from above.
She's filled our lives with happiness
And our hearts full of love.

-Dana Roberts Clark

Peek-a-BOO with bright eyes and pudgy little hands
Calming fears on a first Halloween
when someone says "BOO!"
Kiss a BOO-BOO when a tiny finger gets
caught in a drawer
"You look BOO-tiful Mommy"
on date night with Daddy
"Oops, I made a BOO-BOO" says a tearful voice
when your new plant is smashed on the floor.

BOO-hoo...they're growing up.

-Laura Taylor Mark

You have the face of an angel
With your beautiful smile
No one can resist those eyes—
What undeniable style!

-Linda Price

I look into your eyes and I see
The greatest miracle given to me.
You are the joy of everyday.
Your smile guides my way.

-Shelley Howington

Cherished gift from God above
Hug you tight with all my love
Inspires me to feel young again
Let me always be your friend

-Dana Roberts Clark

When you learned to say, DaDa we were so proud.
When you learned bite and baba, we were wowed.
Now you know most words very well.
Oh, the stories you can tell!

-Shelley Howington

You are my shining moon; you are my glistening sun.
You are my inner peace; you are my abundant fun.
You are my roaming land; you are my wavy sea,
You are, and always will be, everything to me.
-Crystal Dawn Perry

You are my star,
You shine so bright.
When my heart gets dark,
You send me light.
-Dana Roberts Clark

Christmas
(see also Santa Claus)
I've wrapped a hundred presents
and tied as many bows.
I've visited different Santas
and heard the "Ho Ho Ho's".

I've sat through many reruns
but I always shed the tears
when Charlie Brown buys the Christmas tree
or when Frosty disappears.

I've untangled a mile of lights
and decorated a forest of trees.
I have ornaments and Christmas cards,
a supply of reds and greens.

I've spent lots of money on gifts
and waited hours in shopping mall lines.
What I've learned is the power of Christmas
is simply found in a child's eyes.
-Gina Marie Lauchner

The sparkle in my child's eyes,
Of wonder and delight
Shines brighter than any Christmas lights,
Glowing in the night.
-Unknown

'Twas the night before Christmas,
When all through the house
Not a creature was stirring-not even a mouse:
The stockings were hung by the chimney with care,
In hopes that St. Nicholas soon would be there.
-Clement C. Moore

From home to home and heart to heart
From one place to another
The warmth and joy of Christmas
Brings us closer to each other.
-Emily Matthews

Christmas Blessings
Of the heart...
Never shall they fade.

Always I'll remember,
Always I'll treasure,
Christmas memories we've made.
-Najah T. Clemmons

Church

I count down the days: 1,2,3,4,5,6,7
Then we can go to church
And learn about heaven.
Mommy puts us in a dress
And combs our hair just right.
She loads us up in the car
And makes us promise not to fight.
-Dana Roberts Clark

Cooking
Ovens and grills, culinary skills
Food thermometers, appetizers
Washing dishes and wiping up spills
Grating cheese for recipes, slicing and dicing and icing
Fruits and rice and homemade bread
Spice and herbs and sauces
Puree, flambé, scooping, stirring and mixing
Baking a cake, licking the spoon,
There's a lot going on in the kitchen.
-Gina Marie Lauchner

Crafts
Hand made with love from me to you,
I sprinkled warmth and caring into the glue.
So you see with these things holding it together,
It's just like our friendship-
It will last through any weather!
-Laura Taylor Mark

Cute as a button I've always heard
But I've always thought they were just words
Because there's no way a button could be
As cute as you are to me.
-Dana Roberts Clark

Crawling
If anyone tells you,
"Don't come crawling to me,"
You can rest assured
That it won't be me.
-Aparna Iyer

With two hands of butter,
Soft and sweet,
You pat the floor
And slide your knees.

Your bottom goes up,
And your head goes down,
As you try to explore
All that's around.

And as I watch you,
I soon realize
That my very own heart
Is no longer inside.

With your bottom on top,
And your head below,
My heart didn't have
Any place to go,

Than farther and farther
Outside of me,
Chasing your heels
Passionately.

-Aparna Iyer

On your knees, you are
Across the room is very far
One arm first, then your knee
Hey, everybody! Look at me!

-Shelley Howington

I was pregnant then I blinked my eyes...
And I held you in my arms.
I brought you home then I blinked my eyes...
Your first smile showed me your charms.
I watched you crawl then I blinked my eyes...
You're growing so fast; forgive my cries.
I was pregnant then I blinked my eyes.

-Dana Roberts Clark

Crying

Once upon a memory,
Someone wiped away a tear,
Held me close and loved me.
Thank you, Mother dear.

-Unknown

I used to listen to the weather,
But lately I don't seem to care.
Sunshine and rain no longer matter,
Except in the expression you wear.

When raindrops dare to dampen
The sweet windows of your soul,
Washing away your tender tears
Is my most important goal.

And when the sunshine reappears
In your charming, disarming smile,
I know I'll save that warming image,
In my eternal memory file.

-Aparna Iyer

Baby, baby, rock-a-bye.
Baby, baby, please don't cry.
Baby, baby, you are loved.
Angels watch you from above.

-Linda Price
Little Lace Lady, Chattanooga Choo-Choo

Never a lip is
Curved with pain
That can't be kissed
Into smiles again.

-Bret Harte

Dance

I'm practicing in my dancing shoes
In ballet slippers, oh, so new!
I'm holding on to the bar
And stretching my legs so very far.
One day I'll be a dancing star!

-Phyllis Levine

Daughter
(see also Baby, Child, and Girl)

The most precious gift
From Heaven above
Is the gift of a daughter
For a mother to love.

-Dana Roberts Clark

A daughter is a dream come true.
Pink lace, ribbons, fluff and froufrou,
Giggles, kisses, bubbles and bows,
She's such a sweet dear from her head to her toes!

-Laura Taylor Mark.

God did not give me a son
But he did give me you.
You are my little tomboy.
You can do anything boys can do.

-Dana Roberts Clark

Death (special memories)

Mommy, Mommy, please don't cry.
I know you don't understand why
You'll never hold me in your arms.
You'll never see all of my charms.
Never is a word you should never say
Because you can come see me one day.
My Heavenly Father looked at my life;
He saw all the pain and all the strife
So He kept me here with Him to live
And salvation for you He freely gives
So you can come and live here too.
Mommy, please don't cry, I love you.

-Dana Roberts Clark

I cannot see her
But I know she is there.
She's my guardian angel;
My life with me she shares.
Until my time is over
And God wants to bring me home,
She will be there to protect me
When things sometimes go wrong.

-Dana Roberts Clark

Those we love remain with us...
In the whisper of the wind
In a soft rain that falls from heaven
In each sunrise
In every single star that lights the night sky and
In every single memory we hold within our hearts.

-Mary Chandler Huff

Diet

I had an extra piece of cake,
Or maybe two or three.
It wasn't long until the extra pounds
Were easy for me to see.
My clothes are tight, I'm feeling fat.
There is just one thing to do;
I'm going to start a diet
And lose a pound or two.

-Dana Roberts Clark

Dog

Playful and cuddly,
Paws wet and muddy,
Walks in the sunshine,
Barking in the nighttime,
Fur that needs brushing,
Tricks that need working,
Begging and panting,
Scratching and playing
Comforting and petting,
One of the family.

-Gina Marie Lauchner

Doll
I love my baby doll.
I like to serve her tea.
My baby doll is really cute
But she's not as cute as me!
-Crystal Dawn Perry

I always wanted a special doll
With eyes that open and blink at me
To take on trips with my family.
I would dress her like a movie star.
I know her glamour would take her far.
It would be such fun for me to choose
Fancy dresses that match her shoes.
-Phyllis Levine

Dress-up
Twirling, swirling, round and round
In your sparkling princess gown
On your toes, you greet the sky
Kissing heaven, only 2 feet high.
-Julie Perkins Cantrell

Pearls and boas, dressed to the nines,
Lipstick on pursed lips, trying to stay in the lines.
Big wobbly high heels on tiny, precious feet,
Little girls playing dress up - aren't they sweet!
-Laura Taylor Mark

A cape to hide your secret powers
Swords can make you smile for hours
Magic spells and wizard's wand
In far off lands you greet the dawn.
-Julie Perkins Cantrell

Easter

Rainbow colored eggs scattered randomly here and there
Jelly beans, chocolate bunnies and a plush beribboned bear
Children's squeals of delight at baskets overflowing
Their sweet tooth in full gear with chocolate faces glowing.

Giving thanks for all the blessings that we have received
Reflecting on the past year and everything achieved
Dressed in Sunday best clothes, family can be found
At the table for Easter dinner with blessings all around.

-Laura Taylor Mark

It's not the new dress with a matching hat.
It's not all the candy that makes you feel fat.
It's not going to church to hear the bells ring.
It's to celebrate the Holy Risen King!

-Dana Roberts Clark

Eating

The game continues
Every single day.
Baby needs to eat but
Baby wants to play!

-Abby Goldstein Slutsky

Engagement

A world holding two people
So much in love.
A joy that is growing
And blessed from above.
Two people are going
Down the same path together...
A decision—on a mission
To love each other forever.

-Gina Marie Lauchner

40

It's finally happened.
I want the world to know.
I love him with all my heart
And here's my ring to show...
-Dana Roberts Clark

Isn't it amazing to think
It started with a single kiss
And now it's going to end up with
A life of wedded bliss.
-John Beith

Will she say yes, will she say no
How my heart is beating so
I know I want to spend the rest of my life
With her as my partner, my best friend, my wife.
-Dana Roberts Clark

Fall
Pretty colors and
Changing leaves;
That's what autumn
Means to me.
-Dana Roberts Clark

Soothing autumnal days
Fade fast with the shortened
Rays as winter
Descends over the land.
-K B Ballentine

Crunching, crinkling autumn leaves,
Spiraling, swirling in the breeze.

Rake them; pile them; stack them high.
Deep down under there I hide.

Hear my laughter; see my smile.
Hold this memory for a while.

Soon all leaves will blow away
But in your mind, I still will play.

-Julie Perkins Cantrell

Family Tree
(see also Heritage)

One day I sat on Grandma's knee,
I had some questions puzzling me.
"What kind of tree is a family tree?
How tall can it really be?
Does it grow flowers, fruits, or nuts?
Or is it firewood to be cut?"
"Ah my dear," she answered me.
"A family tree is not a tree.
There are no leaves or limbs or bark,
But I won't keep you in the dark.
Think of your aunts, your uncles, your brother,
Even your grandpa, or father and mother,
These are the ones that make up your tree,
Along with your other ancestors, you see.
It's full of love and people who care;
Common roots you all share.
There you go dear-that's your tree."
My grandma stopped and smiled at me.
I grinned back and kissed her cheek,
"Thank you for the answers I seek."

-Margo L. Dill

Picture with me an apple tree;
the fallen apples have passed to eternity,
the mellow apples are living happily,
and the green apples are young and free.
These apples make up my family tree.

-Dana Roberts Clark

Farm

Down on the farm,
What did I see?
A moo cow staring right at me.
Down on the farm,
What did I hear?
A rooster crowing in my ear.
Down on the farm,
After I was done,
I learned a farm is so much fun!

-Dana Roberts Clark

Father

A father is like a lighthouse
Standing tall above the seas.
When the storms of life come crashing in,
The light from your father you'll see.

-Dana Roberts Clark

For all the hugs you've given me
For always making me believe
There were no limits to my dreams
I was always on the winning team
For all I've done, you love me still
How can I tell you all that I feel?
Dad, I love you.

-Dana Roberts Clark

When my life began
You were there...
When I took my first step
You were there...
When I said my first word
You were there...
When I started school
You were there...
When I played ball
You were there...
When I was sick
You were there...
When I broke your hearts
You were there...
When I got in trouble
You were there...
When I needed to talk
You were there...
When I've made mistakes
You've been there...
When I've failed
You've been there...
When I succeeded
You've been there...
There has never been a time
You haven't been there.
How can I begin to tell you
How much I love you and
How thankful I am that
You've always been there.

-Dana Roberts Clark

The greatest gift
I ever had
It came from God
I call him Dad.
-Unknown

Dad, you're the best and at the top of my list.
Just in case I never let you know,
With my whole heart, I love you so!
-Shelley Howington

Run through the house
Jump on my bed
Because I'm playing
With my Dad.
Get in the car
Turn the key
My first time driving
My Dad and me.
Walk me down the aisle
In my pretty white dress.
Please, don't cry, Daddy,
I'll always love you best.
-Dana Roberts Clark

One of the most precious gifts
From Heaven above
Is the gift of a daughter
For a Daddy to love.
-Dana Roberts Clark

A tower of strength when things go wrong
Understanding when the road is long
That is what puts daddies above the rest
And to me Daddy you are the best.
-Dana Roberts Clark

I've been blessed to have
a Daddy like you.
You're my pal, my buddy,
and my best friend too.

-Dana Roberts Clark

It's honey do this and Daddy do that
Please put up the dishes and give the kids a bath.
I know sometimes I act like I don't see
But you're the best husband and Daddy you could be.

-Dana Roberts Clark

Fishing

Going fishing
Gonna take a day
To get in touch
The old fashioned way

Don't need much
Just a pole and line
Gonna dig some worms
And let life untwine.

-Brenda Darlene Kijowski

It's easy to get hooked on fishing
But it's hard to get the fish.
We spend a lot of time wishing
That our big chance wasn't missed.
Trying to lour the big one
Sitting patiently for hours
Fishing can be so much fun
Unless the fish have all the power!

-Gina Marie Lauchner

Flowers/Gardening

May you grow deep and independent roots.

May your soil be blessed with peace,
where life in all its forms will comfort you.

May your stems stand sturdily against the wind and rain,
and may they reach high toward an open sky.

May your vines become entwined,
offering support to one another.
May your leaves be richly filled with nourishment
for your souls.

May your flowers display a beautiful palette
as they worship the sun and all that nature offers.

May you enjoy the seasons of your lives together;
the promise of Spring, the warmth of Summer,
the reflection of Autumn, and the calm of Winter.

May your beauty and grace bring smiles to children's faces,
memories to aged hands, and a solace to broken hearts.

May you always grow in spirit and in love.

Life is but a garden.

May yours endure a long and fruitful season.
-Julie Perkins Cantrell

Pansies with their smiling faces eagerly await,
As ivy tendrils dance merrily around the garden gate.
Roses in their finery are all pretty and abloom.
The dance has just begun in my backyard ballroom.
-Laura Taylor Mark

If sisters were flowers,
I'd still pick you.
I'd let the sun shine
So you'd never be blue.
I'd show the world
How beautifully you grew
With bright bold colors and
Strength through and through.
If sisters were flowers,
I'd pick you right away
Because you cheer me up
And bring smiles each day.
If sisters were flowers,
For what it's worth,
I'd always pick you
-The best sister on Earth.
-Gina Lauchner

Freckles

I love your freckles, little one.
They are beautiful to me.
I can't think of anything
More beautiful to see.
-Brenda Darlene Kijowski

Just name me one thing prettier
Than freckles that you know.
And the little boy just smiled, and
Whispered, "Wrinkles when they glow."
-Brenda Darlene Kijowski

Friend

Count your blessings, not your crosses,
Count your gains, not your losses.
Count your joys instead of your woes,
Count your friends instead of your foes.
Count your health, not your wealth.

-Old Proverb

Our friendship is a jewel,
one of the rarest kind.
A treasure most cherished,
the best you'll ever find.
One of the most precious gifts
you could ever receive.
For the bonding of two hearts,
is not easy to achieve.

-Mary Chandler Huff

A friend will give you comfort
and hours on the phone.
A friend knows when you need a hug
or want to be left alone.

A friend knows when you need an ear
to just sit there and listen.
A friend helps you to calm your fears,
and cheers on your ambitions.

A friend can make you laugh out loud
even when there's no one around
A friend is someone who makes you proud
of the friend that you have found.

-Gina Marie Lauchner

A friend is there for you every day.
They know you as you are...
and love you anyway.
-Mary Chandler Huff

Friend (long distance)
Separated by distance
My friend, you and me
But you brighten my life
I am thankful for thee.
-Brenda Darlene Kijowski

Girl/Girls
There is nothing like a little girl.
She will brighten up your whole world.
With her beautiful eyes and long curls,
She is more precious than any pearls.
-Dana Roberts Clark

She's a little touch of heaven
Sent down from above.
She's filled our lives with happiness
And our hearts full of love.
-Dana Roberts Clark

Little girls with pretty curls
Oh, how cute they are!
Maybe when they grow up
Some day they will be a star!
-Linda Price

Twirling, swirling, round and round
In your sparkling princess gown
On your toes, you greet the sky
Kissing heaven, only 2 feet high.
-Julie Perkins Cantrell

Girl Scouts

When you're part of a Girl Scout troop,
You're a member of a special group;
One that cares about society's youth
And imparts values like honor and truth.

When you take the oath and become a Girl Scout,
The smile in your pocket should always come out.
You learn ways to overcome fear and doubt
and what being a good person is all about.

You get to go camping and learn the best way to pack.
You hear ghost stories and share lots of laughs.
You might hike and then learn how to find your way back
Or learn to tie knots, and do arts and crafts.

You may learn about nature, birds and plants
And what to do for injuries and poison ivy rash.
You sell cookies and learn fundraising and finance,
And every Girl Scout learns how to sew their own patch.

-Gina Marie Lauchner

Golf

Of COURSE everyone is GREEN at one time
or another but the HOLE idea is to feel the
DRIVE and not just PUTTER around.
WOOD you rather have a CHIP on your
shoulder or fly on the EAGLEs wings?
Don't just CART around your BAG of
BELOW PAR scores,
FORE you are bound for SAND TRAPS.
Join the CLUB. Have a BALL, and seek
IRONy in life. The early BIRDie gets the worm.
Don't get TEEd off! Just remember what
BOGEY Beara might've said,
"Put the heart before the GOLF COURSE."

-Gina Marie Lauchner

Graduation

The future is as bright
as the student looking towards it.
The only thing standing in the way
on graduation day is a tassel
that tickles a shining face;
and twinkling eyes so full of grace.
The future is as bright
as my child looking towards it
Nothing stands in the way
of a beautiful graduation day.

-Gina Marie Lauchner

I have waited for this day with sweet anticipation.
The joy and pride that fills my heart has been
my revelation,
That you are indeed an extraordinary young man,
a blessing beyond explanation.
So here before you I proudly stand and as I struggle to
let go of your hand,
I pray...
That God will watch over you no matter where you go,
That you will never loose your balance no matter how
hard the wind may blow.
That you always remember home and the love that we
have for you,
And that you always give glory to God for all that he
will enable you to do.

Congratulations my beautiful son...
your day has come.

-Lisa M. Billings

Fifteen years ago you were only three,
growing more and more curious of the world around
you each day. You were my precious baby boy and the
thought of you some day becoming a young man was
so far away.

Ten years ago you were only eight,
growing more independent, becoming more perceptive
of the world around you each day. A baby boy you
were no more. Still, the thought of you graduating
high school; making decisions without me, was
something too far down the road to look for.

Five years ago you were thirteen,
growing more precocious, with such self-awareness
that would sometimes leave me speechless.
I knew that my baby boy was growing up,
but part of me was not ready nonetheless.

Today you are eighteen,
and this is just the beginning for you.
I cannot hold your hand anymore
to keep you safe while crossing the street.
I cannot tell you not to tell you whom you should trust
and not trust out of the many you will meet.

Because today you are eighteen,
when just the other day you were three.
Once my baby boy and now my young man,
I thank God for all of those years and the blessing
of you that he has given me.

Congratulations!
-Lisa M. Billings

Today a dream is coming true.
A world of possibility lies ahead for you.
Look back with me over 18 years-
We've shared a lot of happiness, joys, and tears.
I pray I've given you all you have needed
Because today, finally, you have succeeded.
When you walk across the platform today,
Know all my pride and love go with you
Every step of the way.

-Dana Roberts Clark

Grandchildren

A copy of a copy
Will surely disappoint.
Videos and documents
Are cases in point.

The only time an original
Should be copied twice,
Is when a person
Is especially nice.

That person needs to make
A baby-faced clone,
And that clone should make another
Clone of her own.

The result will truly be
A spectacular sight,
For this copy of a copy
Will be a grand delight!

-Aparna Iyer

I was pregnant then I blinked my eyes...
And I held you in my arms.
I brought you home then I blinked my eyes...
Your first smile showed me your charms.
I watched you crawl then I blinked my eyes...
And you were running down the hall.
Your first day at school then I blinked my eyes...
I heard your first boyfriend call.
Sweet sixteen came then I blinked my eyes...
Your dad bought you an old car.
Your college life began then I blinked my eyes...
You've always been our shining star.
Dad walked you down the aisle then I blinked my eyes.
You've grown up so fast forgive my cries.
You are pregnant then I blinked my eyes...

-Dana Roberts Clark

Grandfather
(see also Grandparents)

They searched the heavens, near and far;
Inside each cloud, on every star.
To heavens all, a sad dismay;
A special angel had gone astray.
The Lord did finally look on down,
And see a twinkle on this ground.
A message rose from earth that day,
As Grandpa smiled up to say;
"I'm here, My Lord, do not dismay,
This angel has not gone astray."

-Brenda Darlene Kijowski

I've been blessed to have
a Papaw like you.
You're my pal, my buddy,
and my best friend too.

-Dana Roberts Clark

A grandpa is made by God's precious hands
He lovingly stitches each and every strand.
A grandpa is more precious than silver or gold
And wise beyond belief with his stories of old.
A grandpa always know exactly what to say
To give you peace in your heart
And brighten your day.
If we did not have a grandpa
Where would we be?
Because everyone loves their grandpa-
Including me!

-Dana Roberts Clark

Grandmother
(see also Grandparents)

A grandma is made by God's precious hands.
He lovingly stitches each and every strand.
A grandma is more precious than silver or gold
And wise beyond belief with her stories of old.
A grandma always know exactly what to say
To give you peace in your heart
And brighten your day.
If we did not have a grandma
Where would we be?
Because everyone loves their grandma-
Including me!

-Dana Roberts Clark

Grandmas. . .
Smell like chocolate chip cookies;
Bake better than Betty Crocker;
Hug as if there's no tomorrow;
Love like you're an angel-
Even when you aren't.

-Margo L. Dill

They searched the heavens, near and far;
Inside each cloud, on every star.
To heavens all, a sad dismay;
A special angel had gone astray.
The Lord did finally look on down,
And see a twinkle on this ground.
A message rose from earth that day,
As Grandma smiled up to say;
"I'm here, My Lord, do not dismay,
This angel has not gone astray."

-Brenda Darlene Kijowski

Grandparents
(see also Grandfather and Grandmother)

Just name me one thing prettier
Than freckles that you know.
And the little boy just smiled, and
Whispered, "Wrinkles when they glow."

-Brenda Darlene Kijowski

You are a unique treasure
A trusted friend and loved ally
As grandparents, you are unequalled,
My rainbow in the sky.

-Brenda Darlene Kijowski

Growing up

As you slept tonight, all cozy in your bed,
I peeked in on you and kissed your little head.
I thought of all the hopes and dreams that I have for you.
Will I ever feel I've done everything I could do?

You're growing up so fast; time is stealing you away
I feel it when you blow a kiss and head to school every day.
If only time would stand still for mothers everywhere
So they could hold onto their kids,
And keep them in their care.

Today I'm happy for the clutter and toys strewn about
I'm treasuring each memory, first smile, tooth and pout.
Tomorrow will be here in the blink of an eye
And I'll be wishing it all back when you grow up and say,
"Good-bye."

-Laura Taylor Mark

I was pregnant then I blinked my eyes
And I held you in my arms.
I brought you home then I blinked my eyes
Your first smile showed me your charms.
I watched you crawl then I blinked my eyes
And you were running down the hall.
Your first day at school then I blinked my eyes
I heard your first boyfriend call.
Sweet sixteen came then I blinked my eyes
Your dad bought you an old car.
Your college life began then I blinked my eyes
You've always been our shining star.
Dad walked you down the aisle then I blinked my eyes
You've grown up so fast forgive my cries.
You are pregnant then I blinked my eyes...

-Dana Roberts Clark

Another inch taller
Another shoe size too small
Another grade that passes
New supplies for new classes
Another book that is read
New words to comprehend
Another birthday gift opened
Another day I am hoping
Another tear in my eye
Will slow these years going by.

-Gina Marie Lauchner

Gymnastics

Flip-flops, dismounts, leaps and turns
Cartwheels, balance beams, routines to learn
Backbends, somersaults, pointing your toes
Practicing form for the perfect pose.
Twisting and turning and spinning around
Vaulting and jumping then landing on the ground
Handsprings and handstands, ice packs and heat
The life of a gymnast just can't be beat.

-Gina Marie Lauchner

Hair

Split-ended, bed-headeded, in need of a trim,
Blow-dried, sun-fried, tangled in the wind,
Flat or frizzy, curly, unruly,
Smooth, shampooed, conditioned,
A hair-do never looks like new
So let's just call it a hair-did.

-Gina Marie Lauchner

The perfect hairstyle is sleek, long, and trim,
Or maybe it's soft and falls in nice waves,
For certain, the style will cause her to slave.

For the style she chooses is not what nature provides,
But dryers and curlers, and all sorts of dyes,
Will make it seem natural in somebody's eyes.

-Abby Goldstein Slutsky

Halloween

Peek-a-BOO with bright eyes and pudgy little hands
Calming fears on a first Halloween when someone says"BOO!"
Kiss a BOO-BOO when a tiny finger gets caught in a drawer
"You look BOO-tiful Mommy" on date night with Daddy
"Oops, I made a BOO-BOO" says a tearful voice when your
new plant is smashed on the floor.
BOO-hoo...they're growing up.

-Laura Taylor Mark

It's the time when monsters knock on your door
and you don't even question what they've come for.
When pumpkins have faces and faces have masks
and children get candy without even having to ask.
It's the time when goblins can be found on the street
and ghosts and witches say "trick-or-treat!"
It's the time to decorate with oranges and blacks,
go to a haunted house, hayride or pumpkin patch.
It's the time to dress up like a clown or a cat,
a caveman or princess or vampire bat.
It's the time that comes at the end of October,
and it's time to get more candy before
Halloween is over!

-Gina Marie Lauchner

Heritage

*Whether a family is bound together
or scattered far apart,
Loved ones from the past and present
are always in our heart.
Legacies of love and pride are passed down
through the years,
Journals kept of triumphs, tragedies and tears.
Tales of great joy, sacrifice and sorrow can be found,
Character traits, personalities and likenesses abound.
Families give us history, roots tied to our past
And a heritage that's honored is one that's sure to last.*

-Laura Taylor Mark

*The handing down of knowledge
from generations unsurpassed,
Beliefs and customs taught,
strongly rooted in our past.*

*Linking our tomorrows with
the treasures of yesterday.
A precious gift that can be cherished
and shared along the way.*

-Brenda Darlene Kijowski

Home/House

*Every spot in this house holds some meaning-
every corner, every wall, all the floors and the ceiling.
Every room conjures up its own special feeling.
I love this house, though it might need some cleaning!*

-Gina Marie Lauchner

May each soul that steps inside
Feel the joy where love abides
And the warmth of Gods true love
He sends us freely from above.

-Mary Huff Chandler

Hug

Happiness when you give one
Understanding when you need one
Great when you receive one

-Dana Roberts Clark

Hunting

Not just anyone can be a hunter.
It takes a certain kind.
It's not for the squeamish or fearful,
or those with a weak mind.

You've got to have the right tools
and know just how to use them.
You've got to know the rules,
and never try to abuse them.

Not just anyone can be a hunter.
It requires certain skills;
common sense and patience,
and a hand that is steady and still.

Some choose hunting for sport, for fresh air or fun
Some hunt for food and survival.
But whoever becomes a hunter
plays a role in the world's life cycle.

-Gina Marie Lauchner

Dressed in camouflage
As if he goes to war,
I see the hunter trod
Into the field, once more.

I hear the warriors cry
And the beating of the drums,
As he passes back in time
From whence, we all did come.

-Brenda Darlene Kijowski

Husband

(see also Anniversary, Love and Wedding)

It's honey do this and Daddy do that
Please put up the dishes and give the kids a bath.
I know sometimes I act like I don't see
But you're the best husband and Daddy you could be.

-Dana Roberts Clark

Big, strong shoulders to hold all your cares,
Back rubber, bath scrubber, fixer of creaky stairs,
The man of your dreams, asleep or awake,
The butter on your biscuit; the icing on your cake.
He's the man you've chosen to share your life
He's your ever-loving husband and you're
his proud wife!

-Laura Taylor Mark

Illness

This sickness has no boundaries
No oceans it won't cross
An illness that's invisible
Submerged in utter chaos.

-Brenda Darlene Kijowski

Vaccinations, constipation,
Sprains and splints and splinters
Indigestion, lozenges, Kleenex, gauze and fevers
Contusions and concussions, band-aids and bruises
Nausea and stomach aches and scrapes
And stuffed-up noses
Bacteria, infections, strep throat
And stings and stitches
Laryngitis, penicillin, bumps and hives and itches
Chills and pills and viruses, vitamins, dehydration
Antiseptic, dizzy spells, bites and allergic reactions
Doctor appointments, eye drops and ointments
Cough medicine and wheezing
Chicken soup and colds and flus
Ice packs, swelling and sneezing...

-Gina Marie Lauchner

Independence Day

July sizzles and pops
With red, white, and blue rockets;
Gold sparklers in one hand and poppers in the other—
Deep, dark nights lit with riotous color.

-K B Ballentine

R*emembering*
E*arly*
D*ays*

W*hen*
H*aving*
I*ndependence*
T*hreatened*
E*nemies...*

A*merican*
N*oblemen's*
D*eclaration*

B*ecame*
L*iberty,*
U*nity,*
E*quality.*

-Gina Marie Lauchner

Injury

Peek-a-BOO with bright eyes and pudgy little hands
Calming fears on a first Halloween when someone says
"BOO!"
Kiss a BOO-BOO when a tiny finger gets caught in a drawer
"You look BOO-tiful Mommy" on date night with Daddy
"Oops, I made a BOO-BOO" says a tearful voice when your
new plant is smashed on the floor.

BOO-hoo...they're growing up.

-Laura Taylor Mark

When you hurt yourself
it's like I feel it, too.
I want to take the pain away;
to take it away for you.
-Gina Marie Lauchner

Vaccinations, constipation,
Sprains and splints and splinters
Indigestion, lozenges, Kleenex, gauze and fevers
Contusions and concussions, band-aids and bruises
Nausea and stomach aches and scrapes
And stuffed-up noses
Bacteria, infections, strep throat
And stings and stitches
Laryngitis, penicillin, bumps and hives and itches
Chills and pills and viruses, vitamins, dehydration
Antiseptic, dizzy spells, bites and allergic reactions
Doctor appointments, eye drops and ointments
Cough medicine and wheezing
Chicken soup and colds and flus
Ice packs, swelling and sneezing...
-Gina Marie Lauchner

Inspirational
Reach high!
The best is always kept
upon life's topmost shelves,
but not beyond our reach
if we will reach beyond ourselves.
-Brenda Darlene Kijowski

Count your blessings, not your crosses,
Count your gains, not your losses.
Count your joys instead of your woes,
Count your friends instead of your foes.
Count your health, not your wealth.
-Old Proverb

Reach high,
For stars lie hidden in your soul.
Dream deep,
For every dream precedes the goal.

-Pamela Vaull Starr

Kiss
My heart, I'll send to thee.
Wisps of color in the air;
Butterflies from me.

They travel on a gentle breeze
To wherever you may be.
Painting hearts with kisses
Just as those you've sent to me.

-Brenda Darlene Kijowski

Never a lip
Is curved with pain
That can't be kissed
Into smiles again.

-Bret Harte

Kite
The wind is right.
The sky is blue.
A perfect time
To kite with you.
Run down the hill.
The string unwinds.
Up, up and away!
Leave your cares behind.

-Dana Roberts Clark

Love

The loving times we share,
The special things we do,
Are a warm and gentle reminder
Of how much I love you.

-John Beith

Destiny brought you into my life.
I have never felt a love so right.
You are the half that makes me whole.
You are the one who fills my soul.

-Dana Roberts Clark

Marriage is more than just the word love
It is trust, honesty, and friendship-
Gifts sent from Heaven above.

-Dana Roberts Clark

The things I see when I look into your eyes:

I see someone who goes as deep as an ocean,
with its depth, its strength and tremendous emotion.

I see someone, whose heart is as wide as the sky,
so open and so free to whomever passes by.

I see someone, whose soul is as pure as the driven snow,
with honesty and trusting that continues to grow.

I see someone, whose love is as genuine as gold,
so precious and full of value that will never grow old.

Can you imagine? Do you even know why?
These are the things I see when I look into your eyes.

-Lisa M. Billings

I never knew three little words
Could ever mean so much
Until I looked into your eyes
And felt your sweet soft touch.
"I love you."

-Dana Roberts Clark

I've read stories of true love
But I just didn't believe
That fairytales could come true.
I thought it was fantasy
But when I look into your eyes
You are all my dreams come true.
I feel like I can do anything
Anytime I am with you.
It's everything about you
That brings a smile to my face.
Your kind and gentle nature
Makes my heart skip a pace.

-Dana Roberts Clark

It's so easy to love you.
I'm so proud of all you do.
-Shelley Howington

I'm glad
I took a chance
And followed my heart-
Because it led me to yours.

-John Beith

I look into your eyes and I see
The greatest miracle given to me.
You are the joy of everyday.
Your smile guides my way.
-Shelley Howington

I loved you then, I love you now
But time has changed me somehow
The wild and reckless love I felt
The way you made my heart melt
Has slipped away through the years
We've both cried many tears
But the love I feel for you today
Is a better love in every way
Because I know you will be by my side
In your heart I can confide
I love you now, I loved you then
Thank you for being my best friend
-Dana Roberts Clark

Baby, it's you and me
Our love was meant to be
We fit so perfectly
Love for eternity.
-Dana Roberts Clark

I didn't know what to expect
The first time I saw your face
But I fell in love with you instantly.
No one will ever take your place.
-Dana Roberts Clark

You do more than touch me,
You reach me.
You not only look at me,
You see me.
You know who I really am
Not only outside but within.
You not only hear me,
You listen.
-R. Dee Waltz-Daniels

Marines
(see also Military)

They are proud
They are few
They are tough
They are true
They know what to do
for the red, white and blue.

They work hard
They are smart
They have honor
They have heart
The Marines know what to do
They deserve a "thank you!"

-Gina Marie Lauchner

Memories

Those we love remain with us...
In the whisper of the wind
In a soft rain that falls from heaven
In each sunrise
In every single star that lights the night sky and
In every single memory we hold within our hearts.
-Mary Chandler Huff

Military
(see also Army, Marines, and Navy)

Freedom is my greatest asset.
Fear is something I haven't met.

-Shelley Howington

Remember when you held his hand,
And made him groan when asked to stand
Through pledges as we stood and watched
The flag unfurled and staunchly marched?
Remember when he had those fights
And you defended all his rights
And taught him to protect what's his,
And see the world for what it is.
Today your boy is now a man
Who's living all your life commands.
Where once you sheltered as he grew,
He leaves today, to protect you.

-R. Dee Waltz-Daniels

Mother

For all the hugs you've given me
For always making me believe
There were no limits to my dreams
I was always on the winning team
For all I've done, you love me still
How can I tell you all that I feel?
Mom, I love you.

-Dana Roberts Clark

Once upon a memory,
Someone wiped away a tear,
Held me close and loved me.
Thank you, Mother dear.

-Unknown

One of the most precious gifts
From Heaven above
is the gift of a daughter
For a Mother to love.

-Dana Roberts Clark

When my life began
You were there...
When I took my first step
You were there...
When I said my first word
You were there...
When I started school
You were there...
When I played ball
You were there...
When I was sick
You were there...
When I broke your hearts
You were there...
When I got in trouble
You were there...
When I needed to talk
You were there...
When I've made mistakes
You've been there...
When I've failed
You've been there...
When I succeeded
You've been there...
There has never been a time
You haven't been there.
How can I begin to tell you
How much I love you and
How thankful I am that
You've always been there.

-Dana Roberts Clark

God in His wisdom made Mothers
and gave them love to share.
He showed them how to comfort
and told them how to care.
He taught them to wipe a tear
and how to smile just right.
Then He gave them to us
to love with all our might.

-Mary Huff Chandler

Mother-in-law

Our bond wasn't instant
It took a little time
But now I truly love you,
Mother-in-law of mine.

-Dana Roberts Clark

New Year

January peers both forward and back—
Toasting the old and new with
champagne,
friends,
and kisses.

-K B Ballentine

Party

It's not just a regular day
There's gonna be a party
It's time to laugh and play
To get together and be happy

It's not just another day
There's gonna be lots of fun
Celebrate and dance away
The party has begun!

-Gina Marie Lauchner

Pet

You never criticize me
Or get angry when I'm late.
You love it when I hold you
And you never make me wait.

Your love is unconditional
Considerate and kind
And best of all, my precious pet,
I'm yours and you are mine.

-Brenda Darlene Kijowski

Piano

Playing the piano is lots of fun,
Everyone says before the lessons have begun.
Then practicing scales one note at a time,
And trying to remember "Every Good Boy Does Fine".

Even an amateur musician
Requires lots of discipline.
But even Bach and Amadeus
Had to learn the basics!

-Gina Marie Lauchner

When played in combinations
Harmonic music of beauty float
Arousing emotional responses
From hearts with every note.

-Brenda Darlene Kijowski

Prom

Beautiful dress, hair just right,
Glitter, fantasy, a magical night.

Prom night makes a young girl shine,
And feel like floating on cloud nine!

-Laura Taylor Mark

Pumpkin

Pumpkins with their orangey glow
Will soon be sporting faces
As jack-o'-lanterns all aglow
Displayed in many places.

-Laura Taylor Mark

Rain

I used to listen to the weather,
But lately I don't seem to care.
Sunshine and rain no longer matter,
Except in the expression you wear.

When raindrops dare to dampen
The sweet windows of your soul,
Washing away your tender tears
Is my most important goal.

And when the sunshine reappears
In your charming, disarming smile,
I know I'll save that warming image,
In my eternal memory file.

-Aparna Iyer

Rainbow
Whether ye be orange,
or whether ye be green,
Your rainbow has a pot of gold
and shamrocks have four leaves.
Wishes, blarney, little folk,
upon your family tree,
Irish in your history
and luck shall follow thee.

-Brenda Darlene Kijowski

It's said that there is a pot of gold
At the end of each rainbow
But if we spend even one single second
In search of some treasure
We ignore nature's gesture
And risk missing a chance
For an awe-inspiring glance
At true colors embracing the sky...
A rainbow...
Magic, money cannot buy.

-Gina Marie Lauchner

You are a unique treasure
A trusted friend and loved ally
As grandparents, you are unequalled,
My rainbow in the sky.

-Brenda Darlene Kijowski

Retirement
You'll finally have the time to do things you put on hold,
It doesn't mean your life is over,
You're all washed up or old.
It means you've worked hard all your life
And that the time has come
To get out those brushes and paint your future
The journey has just begun!

-Laura Taylor Mark

Rolling Over
I'm pushing up, over, and to the side
I'm rolling over!
Oh, what a ride!
-Dana Roberts Clark

Running
Running away from home
Then running back again.
I start at the same place.
I start right where I end.
-Gina Marie Lauchner

Your cherub-like cheeks
So perfectly round
Your tiny bowed lips
Ready to imitate sounds
Watching your zigzag, wobbly run
I know your learning has just begun.
-Crystal Dawn Perry

Santa Claus
(see also Christmas)
Oh, the wonder in children's eyes
When they finally get to meet
That wondrous fellow who brings the toys
Without missing a beat.
He does his work while we sleep
And in the morning we find out
If he did in fact keep track
Of every good deed, lie or pout.
Who is this guy everyone loves
And who gets no applause?
The one all children will be good for-
Of course, it's Santa Claus!
-Laura Taylor Mark

My sleepy eyes turn bright
When gifts from Santa I see.
Oh! What a sight!
Are ALL these toys for me?

-Crystal Dawn Perry

School

You're growing up so fast; time is stealing you away.
I feel it when you blow a kiss and head to school every day.
If only time would stand still for mothers everywhere
So they could hold onto their kids,
And keep them in their care.

-Laura Taylor Mark

Crayons and markers, papers and pens,
Backpacks and notebooks, counting by tens
School picture time means freshly washed collars
With hard work and patience
They're sure to be scholars!

-Laura Taylor Mark

Another inch taller
Another shoe size too small
Another grade that passes
New supplies for new classes
Another book that is read
New words to comprehend
Another birthday gift opened
Another day I am hoping
Another tear in my eye
Will slow these years going by.

-Gina Marie Lauchner

School (first day)

Timid shoulders holding their shiny new backpack,
Quivering bottom lip makes you want to bring them back
Courageous little boy or brave little miss
You feel your heartstrings pull as you give them a big kiss
And as the teacher guides them they look to you
with tearful eyes
Reminding you it's the first of many firsts
and bittersweet goodbyes

-Laura Taylor Mark

I was pregnant then I blinked my eyes...
And I held you in my arms.
I brought you home then I blinked my eyes...
Your first smile showed me your charms.
I watched you crawl then I blinked my eyes...
And you were running down the hall.
Your first day at school then I blinked my eyes...
You're growing up so fast; forgive my cries.
I was pregnant then I blinked my eyes...

-Dana Roberts Clark

Scrapbooks

Die cuts, vellums and gel pens galore
Fancy papers, awesome borders and stickers to die for
I know I should be doing housework instead
But I've got too many ideas "croppin'" up in my head!

The moment my pages have all been planned
Is when you'll see me take a broom in my hand.
Until then I'm scrappin' and gluing some more
If you come to visit, please don't look at my floor!

-Laura Taylor Mark

Pages filled with laughter
Filled with sorrow
Filled with dreams
Pages that I will cherish forever.

-Najah T. Clemmons

Linking our tomorrows with
The treasures of yesterday.
A precious gift that can be cherished
And shared along the way.

-Brenda Darlene Kijowski

Sing

Hope is the thing with feathers
that perches in the soul
and sings the tune without words
and never stops, at all.

-Emily Dickinson

Sister

A sister is a friend you never knew you had.
She lifts your weary spirits when you're feeling sad.
She somehow finds the words to calm all your fears
And tries to make you smile even through your tears.

A sister is a reflection of us in the mirror,
And as the years go by, similarities are clearer.
For sisters have a tie that is bound with love,
Sharing, caring and blessings from above.

-Laura Taylor Mark

The bond of sisters
Stands the test of time.
I'm so blessed
That you are mine.

-Dana Roberts Clark

Giggles, secrets,
Sometimes tears,
Sisters and Friends
Throughout the years.
-Unknown

My big sister and me
Are two of a kind.
We keep our mother busy
But she doesn't mind.
-Linda Price
Little Lace Lady, Chattanooga Choo-Choo

If sisters were flowers,
I'd still pick you.
I'd let the sun shine
so you'd never be blue.
I'd show the world
how beautifully you grew
with bright bold colors
and strength through and through.
If sisters were flowers,
I'd pick you right away
because you cheer me up
and bring smiles each day.
If sisters were flowers,
for what it's worth,
I'd always pick you
-the best sister on Earth!
-Gina Marie Lauchner

Skateboarding
Knee pads, elbow pads--
Start the show.
Grab your helmet;
Come on, let's go!
-Margo L. Dill

Skating

Creating magic on the ice,
You feel as if you fly;
Painting pictures on frosty glass
With the pressure you apply.

Graceful gliding strokes
With beauty and artistry,
Such overwhelming joy
As skating sets you free.

-Brenda Darlene Kijowski

Knee pads, elbow pads--
Start the show.
Grab your helmet;
Come on, let's go!

-Margo L. Dill

Skiing

Skiing is always a treat;
And a challenge for even an athlete.
There's a time and a place
For such balance and grace,
But just in case
Not everyone is an ace,
And falls flat on their face
In a white-snowed embrace--
It's not a race
Or a high-speed chase
So try to pace yourself;
Have fun and be safe.

-Gina Marie Lauchner

Sleep

I lay you down at night to sleep.
I pray your soul the Lord to keep.
I kiss you and touch your beautiful face.
I know I have you by God's loving grace.

-Shelley Howington

Rest my precious little ones
in peaceful harmony.
The Lord has sent his angels down
to keep watch over thee.
When morning rays
wash over night
and day begins anew;
Wrapped in love
you'll always be
with angel wings round you.

-Brenda Darlene Kijowski

Watching you sleep,
Watching you breathe,
A peaceful end to
Another playful day.
More than a glowing sunset,
More than the shining stars,
You, my little one,
Take my breath away.

-Crystal Dawn Perry

As you slept tonight, all cozy in your bed,
I peeked in on you and kissed your little head.
I thought of all the hopes and dreams that I have for you.
Will I ever feel I've done everything I could do?

-Laura Taylor Mark

Baby, baby, rock-a-bye.
Baby, baby, please don't cry.
Baby, baby, you are loved.
Angels watch you from above.

-Linda Price
Little Lace Lady, Chattanooga Choo-Choo

Smile

You have a unique style
You make everyone smile
A wonderful prize beyond compare
Oh, what a lovely smile you wear!

-Shelley Howington

Today I'm happy for the clutter and toys strewn about
I'm treasuring each memory, first smile, tooth and pout
Tomorrow will be here in the blink of an eye
And I'll be wishing it all back when you grow up and say,
"Good-bye."

-Laura Taylor Mark

I used to listen to the weather,
But lately I don't seem to care.
Sunshine and rain no longer matter,
Except in the expression you wear.

When raindrops dare to dampen
The sweet windows of your soul,
Washing away your tender tears
Is my most important goal.

And when the sunshine reappears
In your charming, disarming smile,
I know I'll save that warming image,
In my eternal memory file.

-Aparna Iyer

You have the face of an angel
With your beautiful smile
No one can resist those eyes—
What undeniable style!

-Linda Price
Little Lace Lady, Chattanooga Choo-Choo

Snow/Winter

The snow is sifting from the sky.
and piling high like a sweet treat from Heaven.
The absence of sound is as soothing to
the soul as the finest symphony.
Peace is all around and for a moment there
are no problems and never were.

-Jo Stack

Dancing in the air
As light as a falling feather
From a birds wing
Falling gently upon my skin
Whispering softly in my ear
Tickling my neck as you land
Twirling in the twilight sky
Mirroring the stars with your grace
Touching the land
Like nothing else can
A blanket of beauty
Pure and soft as I feel you
With my hands and cheeks
As I close my eyes and stare
Far above in the skies, basking
In your tender touch
As magically you embrace me

-Suzanne Smith

Snow silently falling
Nighttime flakes
O'er blanket the
Winter landscape

-K B Ballentine

Snowflakes falling
Winter calling

Zippers zipping
Noses dripping

Mittens warming
Snowmen charming

Sledders racing
Snowballs chasing

Faces chilling
Snowfight thrilling

Ice forts mounding
Snowboots pounding

Mothers calling
Playtime stalling

Snowday ending
Hugs beginning

-Julie Perkins Cantrell

Soccer

I think it's fun.
I think it's neat.
I don't even mind
The scorching heat.
I run up the field,
Chasing after a ball.
I can't use my hands;
That's the rules after all.
I score a goal.
I hear the crowd say,
Hooray! Hooray!
Soccer is so much fun to play!
-Dana Roberts Clark

Son
(see also Baby, Boy, Child)

You've exceeded all my expectations
In all the things you have done
I'm so very proud of you
My one and only son.
-Dana Roberts Clark

One of the most precious gifts
From Heaven above
Is the gift of a son
For a Daddy to love.
-Dana Roberts Clark

Spring

In the silence, my friend,
Listen closely and hear
The secrets that heaven
And earth hold so dear.

The mysterious miracle
That nature will show
If time you will take
To reap what it sows.

Quietly listen
To the sycamore grow,
The snow as it melts
And the stream as it flows.

Quietly listen
As blades of grass wake
When the sun silently dances
Alive on the lake.

Quietly listen
As leaves start to emerge
Enticed by the sunlight
Thrust forward, they surge.

Discover again
In silence review
The mystery and miracle
Of springtime renew.

-Brenda Darlene Kijowski

Star
You are my star,
You shine so bright.
When my heart gets dark,
You send me light.
-Dana Roberts Clark

Reach high,
For stars lie hidden in your soul.
Dream deep,
For every dream precedes the goal.
-Pamela Vaull Starr

St. Patrick's Day
Once when I was kissin'
the blarney stone, ya see'
A wee folk came a sneakin'
round and startled me.
I closed me' eyes
and pinched me'self
and opened them to see,
this leprechaun was sittin' now,
an' laughin' loud at me.
He was no more than
eight inch tall,
potbelly, beard and cap.
Was dressed in green
with golden braid.
A spiffy little chap!
He winked an eye and
puffed his pipe;
then disappeared from view...
but, I heard his Gaelic voice sing out,
Happy St. Patrick's Day to you!
-Brenda Darlene Kijowski

Whether ye be orange,
or whether ye be green,
Your rainbow has a pot of gold
and shamrocks have four leaves.
Wishes, blarney, little folk,
upon your family tree,
Irish in your history
and luck shall follow thee.

-Brenda Darlene Kijowski

Swimming

Jump, Dive, Splish, Splash
"Hey! Watch this!"
Giggle, Scream, Splish, Splash
What an active little fish!

-Crystal Dawn Perry

Swimming through the water
Like a butterfly through air
Or should I say like a monkey...
With limbs flailing here and there!

-Crystal Dawn Perry

Talking

Abba, gaba, hada, raba,
daba, baba, do.
I know sweetheart,
I love you too!

-Dana Roberts Clark

When you learned to say, DaDa we were so proud.
When you learned bite and baba, we were wowed.
Now you know most words very well.
Oh, the stories you can tell!

-Shelley Howington

Teddy Bear
My teddy bear is fluffy and soft
And I love him ever so much.
He cuddles close to me at night
And when he's near all is right.

-Phyllis Levine

Teenager
Red means stop.
Green means go.
I tried to teach you
All that I know.
Now that you're
Behind the wheel,
Before my Father
I will kneel.
I pray that He
Will keep you safe.
Please, be careful,
For everyone's sake.

-Dana Roberts Clark

Sometimes you make me want to scream
Sometimes you make my face beam
Sometimes my patience is very short
But you will always have my love and support.

-Shelley Howington

When you were young, before the "can'ts",
a hundred times, you fell.
But you got up and tried again
until you walked quite well.
But now you say that it's too hard,
too difficult to do.
But what you really mean to say is,
"I simply don't want to."

-Abby Goldstein Slutsky

Thanksgiving

Our blessing are endless
and too many to name
but on Thanksgiving Day
we try just the same.
We want to be sure that
we show the love
that is given to us
from up above.
We smell the aroma
of the feast we can share
and spend Thanksgiving Day
with the ones who are dear.

-Gina Marie Lauchner

Toddler

I was pregnant then I blinked my eyes...
And I held you in my arms.
I brought you home then I blinked my eyes...
Your first smile showed me your charms.
I watched you crawl then I blinked my eyes...
And you were running down the hall.
You're growing so fast; forgive my cries.
I was pregnant then I blinked my eyes.

-Dana Roberts Clark

Your cherub-like cheeks
So perfectly round
Your tiny bowed lips
Ready to imitate sounds
Watching your zigzag, wobbly run
I know your learning has just begun.

-Crystal Dawn Perry

To your guardian Angel,
I have to say...
"Please watch out
for my baby today!"
-Shelley Howington

Toilet Training

I'm so tired, I'm so weary.
Who picked me up and called me "Deary"?
Who sat me on that ol' cold pot
And told me to, when I could not?
I'm not sure but I think it was my mommy.
Mommy! Mommy! I'm through!
-Unknown

You have a small celebration
The first time he uses the commode.
You think "This is going to be easy!"
Then the real nightmare unfolds.
-Dana Roberts Clark

Toys

Today I'm happy for the clutter and toys strewn about
I'm treasuring each memory, first smile, tooth and pout
Tomorrow will be here in the blink of an eye
And I'll be wishing it all back when you grow up and say,
"Good-bye."
-Laura Taylor Mark

Triplets
Three babies to love all at once
A miracle occurred
Endless feedings and diaper changes
Will have to be endured
Three times the attention will need
To be given by loving family
And triple the hugs and kisses
Will be lavished on these three!
-Laura Taylor Mark

Trouble
What is it about trouble
That attracts the brightest and best?
Maybe it just follows us
Maybe it is a test.
Maybe it is hard
To turn the other way
When trouble comes a-knockin'
And wants us to go play.
-Gina Marie Lauchner

Mamma always told me
Trouble was my middle name
But I never understood it
Until a Mother I became.
-Brenda Darlene Kijowski

To your guardian Angel,
I have to say...
"Please watch out
for my baby today!"
-Shelley Howington

Twins
Double the pleasure
Double the fun
Double the chaos
with 2, not just 1.

Double the groceries
Double the food
Double the clothes
They both outgrew.

Double the treasure
It's only just begun
The joy they bring together
will never be outdone.

-Gina Marie Lauchner

Everything in twos, it's a snap to make things match
It's just like making cookies and every time
It's a double batch!

Two of this, two of that and twice the work and fun
Means you've got to start again,
Just as you're almost done!

Double the oohs, two times the aahs and
Twice the well-meaning advice
But two cups of tea and two naps for me
Sure would be oh so nice!

-Laura Taylor Mark

Ultrasound
What a wonderful moment
When you're allowed to view
The precious little package
That's growing inside you.

A glimpse into the future
A miracle in sight
A tiny little baby
An emerging ray of light.

The presence of a miracle
Developing inside
Is only the beginning
Of the joy that coincides.

-Brenda Darlene Kijowski

I heard the sound of your heart,
And my own heart skipped a beat.
There you were, moving around,
In your safe and quiet retreat.

I think I saw your button nose,
Or was that your right ear?
Either way, I know that I
Will hold you near and dear.

I want to tickle those little feet,
That kick me night and day,
I want to hear you coo and cry.
I want to watch you play.

A picture may be worth
A thousand words or more,
But I just can't wait to hold
The little baby I adore.

-Aparna Iyer

I saw you in my tummy today
On a screen of black and white.
The doctor pointed out your parts,
And Daddy's eyes shone bright.
I heard the nurse's voice say,
"Looks like a healthy boy."
A smile broke across my face;
My heart filled with joy.

-Margo L. Dill

Vacation

The places we have gone to
and the trips that we have taken
Photographs of love and laughs
of another family vacation.

It doesn't matter where we go
as long as we're together
At different ages, on these pages-
we'll be on vacation forever.

-Gina Marie Lauchner

Lazy days, fun-filled nights
Dining, shopping, seeing sights
Vacation is the time to do
Whatever brings great joy to you!

-Laura Taylor Mark

Valentine's Day

Love is in the air
More than one day a year
But Valentine's Day
Makes everyone say
"I Love You" to those that are dear.

-Gina Marie Lauchner

Volleyball

Block, bump, spike the ball, direct a cross court attack,
Off the net, center line, send it to the back.

Miss the ball, take a fall and brush the pain aside,
Everyone learns quickly how to swallow pride.

Athletes will do well if they decide when they begin,
Team spirit is important enough
To make them want to win!

-Laura Taylor Mark

Walking

There is no magic day
No way for you to know
No time to take a picture
For you to proudly show
But the memory is forever
Engraved in your mind
When one shaking little leg
Leaves the other leg behind.

-Dana Roberts Clark

The first steps taken after the crawl
The first steps taken towards your first fall
In my arms you once seemed so small
Shall I let go of your hand; should I let go at all?
The first steps taken towards your own will and way
But in my arms is where my heart wants you to stay.

-Gina Marie Lauchner

Wedding
(see also Love)

Run through the house
Jump on my bed
Because I'm playing
With my Dad
Get in the car
Turn the key
My first time driving
My Dad and me
Walk me down the aisle
In my pretty white dress
Please, don't cry, Daddy
I'll always love you best.

-Dana Roberts Clark

A marriage made in heaven
Filled with love and laughter
The kind that only grows and lasts...
Happily ever after.

-Mary Chandler Huff

One day two hearts become one in unity
With patience, love and hard work,
Forever they will be.

-Dana Roberts Clark

My one and only, ever be
with heart and soul
I come to thee.

Thanking you for all you do
with love that beats
forever true.

-Brenda Darlene Kijowski

Marriage is more than just the word love.
It is trust, honesty, and friendship-
Gifts sent from Heaven above.
-Dana Roberts Clark

May you grow deep and independent roots.

May your soil be blessed with peace,
where life in all its forms will comfort you.

May your stems stand sturdily against the wind and rain,
and may they reach high toward an open sky.

May your vines become entwined,
offering support to one another.
May your leaves be richly filled with nourishment
for your souls.

May your flowers display a beautiful palette
as they worship the sun and all that nature offers.

May you enjoy the seasons of your lives together;
the promise of Spring, the warmth of Summer,
the reflection of Autumn, and the calm of Winter.

May your beauty and grace bring smiles to children's faces,
memories to aged hands, and a solace to broken hearts.

May you always grow in spirit and in love.

Life is but a garden.

May yours endure a long and fruitful season.
-Julie Perkins Cantrell

What an honor it is
To witness
The marriage of
Two people in love.
What a way to remind us
Of the miracles
Sent from above.
What a day
To cherish,
To smile, cry, kiss,
To laugh, dance, and hug.
What an honor it is
To celebrate
The marriage of
Two people in love.

-Gina Marie Lauchner

Wife

(see also Anniversary, Love and Wedding)

Wonderful to me you will always be
I can't believe your love for me
Finding you was my greatest feat
Evermore my heart you will keep.

-Shelley Howington

Happy Yesterdays, Happier Tomorrows
Even when life brings us sorrow
With God as my captain and I as your wife
I could not have asked for a better life.

-Dana Roberts Clark

Window

A window is a magic frame
With pictures never twice the same.

It sometimes frames a sunset sky
Where clouds of red and purple fly.

And often when you look at night
It holds the moon and stars so bright.

It's framed a lawn in summer bloom
Where children play and lovers swoon.

Sometimes a tree of gold and red
And grass where crisp leaves are shed.

It sometimes frames a frosty pane
Where snowflakes lite and may remain.

And often it's shown wind blown rain
Pelting against a glassy pane.

A window frames all lovely things
That all the changing seasons bring.

A window is a magic frame
With pictures never twice the same.

-Brenda Darlene Kijowski

Zoo

All the animals we love to see
The lion, the zebra, and the bear under the tree
Blue birds, red birds, orange birds and more
Snakes, turtles, and monkeys galore!

-Shelley Howington

Poems:

Poems:

Poems:

Poems:

One ought, everyday, to hear a song,

read a fine poem, and, if possible,

to speak a few reasonable words.

-Johann Wolfgang von Goethe

Quotes, Crafty sayings, & Scriptures

Adoption

The bond that links your true family is not one of blood, but of respect and joy in each other's life.
-Richard Bach

It is not flesh and blood but the heart which makes us fathers and sons.
-Schiller

The family that you come from isn't as important as the family you're going to have.
-Ring Lardner

Age
(see also Birthday)

Age is a high price to pay for maturity.
-Tom Stoppard

For years I wanted to be older, and now I am.
-Margaret Atwood

You can't help growing older, but you don't have to get old.
-George Burns

Youth comes but once in a lifetime.
-Henry Wadsworth Longfellow

The secret of staying young is to live honestly, eat slowly, and lie about your age.
-Lucille Ball

Nobody loves life like him who is growing old.
-Sophocles

Life begins at forty.
-Walter B. Pitkin

Age is a question of mind over matter.
If you don't mind, it doesn't matter.
-Satchel Paige

I'm over the hill but the climb was terrific!
-Graffiti

The trick is growing up without growing old.
-Casey Stengel

From birth to age 18, a girl needs good parents.
From 18 to 25, she needs good looks.
From 35 to 55, a woman needs personality.
And from 55 on, the old lady needs cash.
-Kathleen Norris

It takes a long time to become young.
-Pablo Picasso

As a white candle in a holy place,
so is the beauty of an aged face.
-Joseph Campbell

It's not the years in your life
but the life in your years that counts.
-Adlai Stevenson

Old age has it's pleasure, which, though different,
are not less than the pleasures of youth.
-W. Somerset Maugham

If wrinkles must be written upon our brows,
let them not be written upon the heart.
The spirit should not grow old.
-James A. Garfield

Live your life and forget your age.
-Frank Bering

Gray hair is a crown of splendor;
it is attained by a righteous life.
Proverbs 16:31

"Keep my commands in your heart,
for they will prolong your life many years
and bring you prosperity,"
says the Lord.
Proverbs 3:1-2

Amusement Park
The only thing we have to fear is fear itself.
-Franklin D. Roosevelt

Feel the fear, and do it anyway
-Susan Jeffers

Angel
Angels are never too shy to tell you that they love you.

Angels sent from up above,
please protect the ones we love...

To every joyous event comes a chorus of angels.

We are each of us angels with only one wing,
and we can only fly by embracing one another.
-Luciano de Crescenzo

If you are seeking creative ideas, go out walking.
Angels whisper to a man when he goes for a walk.
-Raymond Inman

Angels can fly because they take themselves lightly.
-G.K. Chesterton

Every time a bell rings, an angel gets its wings.
-"It's a Wonderful Life"

Music is well said to be the speech of angels.
-Thomas Carlyle

Angels of the Lord,
bless the Lord!
Psalm 148:2

Animals
Of all the animals, the boy is the most unmanageable.
-Plato

Art
To imagine is everything.

Draw a circle, not a heart, around the one you love
because a heart can break but a circle goes on forever.

Life is a great big canvas;
Throw all the paint on it you can.
-Danny Kaye

You have your brush, you have your colors,
you paint paradise, then in you go.
-Nikos Kazantzakis

Art is a higher type of knowledge than experience.
-Aristotle

Art is poetry without words.
-Horace

This world is but a canvas to our imagination.
-Henry David Thoreau

Imagination is more important than knowledge.
Knowledge is limited. Imagination encircles the world.
-Albert Einstein

Art washes away from the soul,
the dust of everyday life.
-Pablo Picasso

The object of art is to give life a shape.
-Jean Anouilh

Each of us is an artist, capable of conceiving and
creating a vision from the depths of our being.
-Dorothy Fadiman

A true work of art is but a shadow
of the divine perfection.
-Michelangelo

There are painters who transform the sun
to a yellow spot, but there are others,
who with the help of their art and their intelligence,
transform a yellow spot into sun.
-Pablo Picasso

Art produces ugly things which
frequently become more beautiful
with time. Fashion, on the other hand,
produces beautiful things which
always become ugly with time.
-Jean Cocteau

Attitude
If you can't change your fate, change your attitude.
-Amy Tan

Baby
(see also Boy, Child, Daughter, Girl, Son, and Toddler)
A baby is a bit of stardust blown from the hand of God!

The greatest miracle of all...

*When they placed you in my arms,
you slipped into my heart.*

*A baby is God's opinion
that the world should go on.*
-Carl Sandburg

Oh, the places you'll go!
-Dr. Seuss

Flowers are words which even a baby can understand.
-Arthur C. Coxe

*Baby's fishing for a dream, Fishing near and far, His
line a silver moonbeam, His bait a silver star.*
-Alice C.D. Riley

*Every child born into the world is a new thought of
God, an ever-fresh and radiant possibility.*
-Kate Douglas Wiggin

*If your baby is...
"beautiful and perfect, never cries or
fusses, sleeps on schedule and burps on
demand, an angel all the time,"
you're the grandma.*
-Theresa Bloomingdale

Children are God's apostles, day by day
sent forth to preach of
love, and hope, and peace.

-James Russell Lowell

The most amazing moment was when he
was handed to me, in his little blanket,
and looked at me with his huge blue eyes.

-Margaret Drabble

Where there is great love,
there are miracles.

-Willa Cather

Life is the first gift,
Love is the second and
Understanding the third.

-Marge Piercy

A new baby is like the beginning of all things -
wonder, hope, a dream of possibilities.

-Eda J. Le Shan

There are no seven wonders of the world
in the eyes of a child. There are seven million.

-Walt Streightiff

There is no other closeness in human life like
the closeness between a mother and her baby:
chronologically, physically, and spiritually,
they are just a few heartbeats away
from being the same person.

-Susan Cheever

There was a star danced, and under that was I born.

-William Shakespeare

There is no place I'd rather be tonight,
except in my mother's arms.
-Duke Ellington

The only way to live is to accept each
minute as an unrepeatable miracle,
which is exactly what is:
a miracle and unrepeatable.
-Storm Jameson

"When the first baby laughed for the first time,
the laugh broke into thousands of pieces
and they all went skipping about,
and that was the beginning of fairies."
(from Peter Pan)

A baby is always more trouble than you thought
-and more wonderful.
-Charles Osgood

Having a baby is like falling in love again,
both with your husband and your child.
-Tina Brown

The infant is music itself.
-Hazrat Inayat Khan

Other things change us,
but we start and end with the family.
-Anthony Brandt

Thanks be to God for his
indescribable gift!
2 Corinthians 9:15

Baptism
(see also Church)
If anyone is in Christ, he is a new creation;
the old has gone, the new has come!
2 Corinthians 5:17

For by grace have you been saved through faith,
and this is not your own doing; it is the gift of God.
Ephesians 2:8

Baseball
(see also Sports)
Take me out to the ballgame,
Take me out to the crowd...

Never let fear of striking out get in your way.
-Babe Ruth

The game is supposed to be fun.
If you have a bad day, don't worry about it.
You can't expect to get a hit every game.
-Yogi Berra

You look forward to it like a
birthday party when you're a kid.
You think something wonderful is going to happen.
-Joe DiMaggio, on Opening Day

Slump ? I ain't in no slump. I just ain't hittin.
-Yogi Berra

The other sports are just sports. Baseball is a love.
-Bryant Gumbel

Life is like a baseball game...
When you think a fastball is coming,
you gotta be ready to hit the curve.
-Jaja Q

You owe it to yourself to be the best you can possible be
-in baseball and in life.
-Pete Rose

Basketball
(see also Sports)
You miss 100% of the shots you don't take.
-Wayne Gretzky

Bath
If children are the ones who take the baths,
why are moms the ones who get soaking wet?

Everything is miraculous.
It is miraculous that one does not melt in one's bath.
-Pablo Picasso

I believe in getting into hot water;
it keeps you clean.
-G.K. Chesterton (1874 - 1936)

Beach
You, me, and the deep blue sea...

And the sea will grant each man new hope,
as sleep brings dreams of home.
-Christopher Columbus

My eyes are an ocean
in which my dreams are reflected.
-Anna Uhlich

My life is like a stroll upon the beach,
as near the ocean's edge as I can go.
-Henry David Thoreau

Surprisingly lively, precious days.
What is there to say except: here they are.
Sifting through my fingers like sand.
-Joyce Carol Oates

The sea does not reward those who are
too anxious, too greedy, or too impatient.
-Anne Morrow Lindbergh

We ourselves feel that what we are doing
is just a drop in the ocean
but the ocean would be less because of
that missing drop.
-Mother Teresa

Men seek out retreats for themselves in the country,
by the seaside, on the mountains...
but all this is unphilosophical to the last degree...
when thou canst at a moment's notice retire into thyself.
-Marcus Aelius Aurelius

Hurt not the earth, neither the sea, not the trees.
Revelations 7:3

Beauty

Beauty is whatever gives joy.
-Hugh Nibley

Beauty is the promise of happiness.
-Henri B. Stendhal

Never lose an opportunity of seeing anything
that is beautiful; for beauty is God's handwriting
...thank God for it.
-Ralph Waldo Emerson

A girl is ...
Innocence playing in the mud,
Beauty standing on its head, and
Motherhood dragging a doll by the foot.
-Allan Beck

A thing of beauty is a joy forever.
Its loveliness increases;
it will never pass into nothingness.
-John Keats

Beauty is not caused. It is.
-Emily Dickinson

And all the loveliest things there be come simply,
so it seems to me.
-Edna St. Vincent Millay

Beauty seen is never lost; God's colors all are fast.
-John Greenleaf Whittier

Beauty is power; a smile is its sword.
-Charles Reade

Beauty of style and harmony and grace and good rhythm depend on simplicity.
-Plato

I praise you because
I am fearfully and wonderfully made;
your words are wonderful, I know that full well.
Psalm 139:14

How beautiful you are, my darling!
Oh, how beautiful! Your eyes are doves.
Song of Songs 1:15

Bird
The bird of paradise alights
only upon the hand that does not grasp.
-John Berry

The woods would be a very silent place
if no birds sang except those that sang best.
-Henry Van Dyke

Birthday
(see also Age)
Grow old along with me! The best is yet to be.
-Robert Browning

The secret of happiness is to count your blessings
-not your birthdays.
-Shannon Rose

Everyone is the age of their heart.
-Guatemalan saying

*How old would you be
if you didn't know how old you were?*
-Satchel Paige

*The real secret of happiness is not what you
give or receive; it's what you share.*
-Unknown

Growing old is mandatory; growing up is optional.
-Unknown

Boat
*I am not afraid of storms,
for I am learning how to sail my ship.*
-Louisa May Alcott

Books
He that loves reading has everything within his reach.

*We shouldn't teach great books,
we should teach a love of reading.*
-B.F. Skinner

Today a reader, tomorrow a leader.
-W. Fusselman

*The beauty of the written word is that it can be
held close to the heart and read over and over again.*
-Florence Littauer

Boxing
(see also Sports)
*You can either stand up and be counted
or lie down and be counted out.*

Boy/Boys

One good reason why a little boy gets so dirty,
he's closer to the ground.

Snips and snails and puppy dogs' tails,
that's what little boys are made of.

Of all the animals, the boy is the most unmanageable.
-Plato

A boy's will is the wind's will,
and the thoughts of youth are long, long thoughts.
-Henry Wadsworth Longfellow

Boys are beyond the range of anybody's sure understanding,
at least when they are between 18 months and 90 years old.
-James Thurber

It's not the men in my life;
it's the life in my men
-Mae West

He has the spirit of the sun,
The moods of the moon,
The will of the wind.
-Julie Perkins Cantrell

What makes a boy more brilliant
than being a grandson?
-Tom Berg

To become a real boy, you must prove yourself
brave, truthful and unselfish.
-from "Pinochio"

Boys will be boys, and so will a lot of middle-aged men.
-Kin Hubbard

Break-up

*'Tis better to have loved and lost
than never to have loved at all.*
-Alfred, Lord Tennyson

*If love is the answer,
could you please rephrase the question?*
-Lily Tomlin

*Tell me why love cannot be
like all the songs that sing to me?*
-Dana Roberts Clark

Heartbreak is life educating us.
-George Bernard Shaw

Brother

A brother is a friend given by Nature.
-Legouve

Those who tease you, love you.
-Jewish proverb

*There is a destiny that makes us brothers;
no one goes his way alone.*
-Edwin Markham

*It is because we are different
that each of us is special.*
-Brian Dyson

*How good and pleasant it is when
brothers live together in unity!*
Psalm 133:1

Butterfly

What the caterpillar calls the end of the world,
the master calls a butterfly.
-Richard Bach

Happiness is a butterfly, which, when pursued,
is always just beyond your grasp, but which,
if you will sit down quietly, may alight upon you.
-Nathaniel Hawthorne

Cars/Driving

The best way to keep children at home is
to make the home atmosphere pleasant
-and let the air out of their tires.
-Dorothy Parker

You know your children are growing up
when they stop asking you
where they came from and refuse to tell
you where they're going.
-P.J. O'Rourke

Never lend your car to anyone
to whom you have given birth.
-Erma Bombeck

One hundred years from now, it will not matter what my
bank account was, how big my house was, or what kind of
car I drove. But the world may be a little better, because I
was important in the life of a child.
-Forest Witcraft

What America needs is more young people
who will carry to their jobs the same
enthusiasm for getting ahead that
they display in traffic.
-Unknown

Cat

Cats are angels with fur.

Time spent with cats is never wasted.

The cat who doesn't act finicky
soon loses control of his owner.
-Morris the Cat

As every cat owner knows, nobody owns a cat.
-Ellen Perry Berkeley

People who love cats have
some of the biggest hearts around.
-Susan Easterly

It is impossible to keep a straight face
in the presence of one or more kittens.
-Cynthia E. Varnado

Child/Children
(see also Baby, Boy, Daughter, Girl, Son and Toddler)

Blessed are the children...
for theirs is a world of wonder.

To our children, we give two things;
one is roots, the other wings

A mother's heart is a special place
where children can always go home.

A child's love is like the dawn unfolding...
bright, new and full of hope.

A mother's children are portraits of herself.

It is not a slight thing when they,
who are so fresh from God, love us.
-Charles Dickens

You brighten my life through storm and rain
Like a million stars shining...forever.
-Najah T. Clemmons

A child is the greatest poem ever known.
-Christopher Morley

While we try to teach our children all about life,
our children teach us what life is all about.
-Angela Schwindt

Don't judge each day by the harvest you reap,
but by the seeds you plant.
-Robert Louis Stevenson

A mother's love is an eternal flame,
forever sparked by her children's own.
-Suzanne Smith

Hang around doggies and kids; they know how to play.
-Geoffrey Godbey

A thing of beauty is a joy forever.
-John Keats

Family faces are magic mirrors.
Looking at people who belong to us,
we see the past, present and future.
-Gail Lumet Buckley

*Pretty much all the honest truth telling
in the world is done by children.*
-Oliver Wendell Holmes

Youth comes but once in a lifetime.
-Henry Wadsworth Longfellow

*Blessed be childhood,
which brings down something of heaven
into the midst of our rough earthiness.*
-Henri Frederic Amiel

*There never was a child so lovely
but his mother was glad to get him asleep.*
-Ralph Waldo Emerson

*When you're young, the silliest notions
seem the greatest achievements.*
-Pearl Bailey

*We never know the love of our parents for us
until we become parents.*
-Henry Ward Beecher

A mother understands what a child does not say.
-Jewish proverb

A father sees himself in his child's eyes.
-Alexander Wood

*Children have never been very good at
listening to their elders, but they have
never failed to imitate them.*
-James Baldwin

Children love to be alone because alone is where they know themselves, and where they dream.
-Roger Rosenblatt

Of all nature's gifts to the human race, what is sweeter to a man than his children?
-Marcus Tullius Cicero

One hundred years from now, it will not matter what my bank account was, how big my house was, or what kind of car I drove. But the world may be a little better, because I was important in the life of a child.
-Forest Witcraft

That great Cathedral space which was childhood.
-Virginia Woolf

Enjoy the little things in life, for one day you will look back and realize they were the big things.
-Unknown

Children are like windows that open onto the future as well as the past, the external world as well as our own private landscapes.
-Jane Swigart

There is always one moment in childhood when the door opens and lets the future in.
-Graham Greene

Surprisingly lively, precious days. What is there to say except: here they are. Sifting through my fingers like sand.
-Joyce Carol Oates

*It is because we are different
that each of us is special.*
-Brian Dyson

The soul is healed by being with children.
-Fyodor Dostoevsky

Children are poor men's riches.
-English Proverb

Raising kids is part joy and part guerilla warfare.
-Ed Asner

*Who takes the child by hand,
takes the mother by the heart.*
-Danish proverb

Safe, for a child, is his father's hand, holding him tight.
-Pam Brown

*If it were going to be easy to raise kids,
it wouldn't have started with something called labor.*
-Unknown

*Every child born into the world is a new thought of God,
an ever-fresh and radiant possibility.*
-Kate Douglas Wiggin

*The work will wait while you show the child the rainbow;
but the rainbow won't wait while you do the work.*
-Patricia Clafford

Children are a bridge to heaven.
-Persian proverb

Children in a family are like flowers in a bouquet:
there's always one determined to face in an opposite
direction from the way the arranger desires.

-Marcelene Cox

Behold, children are a blessing from the Lord.

Psalm 127:3

For where your treasure is,
there will your heart be also.

Matthew 6:21

Her children arise up, and call her blessed.

Proverbs 31:28

Christmas

Guardian angel pure and bright...
please lead Santa here tonight

He who has no Christmas in his heart
will never find Christmas under a tree.

Happiness is a homespun Christmas!

At Christmas,
Play and make good cheer,
For Christmas comes but once a year.

-Thomas Tusser

Love's the thing. The rest is tinsel.

-Pam Brown

Christmas is the day that holds all time together.

-Alexander Smith

The real secret of happiness is not what you
give or receive; it's what you share.
-Unknown

I will honor Christmas in my heart,
and try to keep it all the year.
-Charles Dickens

May you have the gladness of Christmas, which is
hope; The spirit of Christmas, which is peace;
The heart of Christmas, which is love.
-Ada V. Hendricks

Merry Christmas to all and to all a good night!
-Santa Claus

Christmas Cheer Recipe -
Combine loads of good wishes,
heartfuls of love and armfuls of hugs.
Sprinkle with laughter and garnish with mistletoe.
Top off with presents. Serves everyone!
-Unknown

For unto us a child is born,
unto us a son is given.
Isaiah 9:6

Glory to God in the highest,
and on earth peace,
good will toward men.
St. Luke 2:14

Church
(see also Baptism)
The soul is awakened through service.
-Erica Jong

Only God knows where you are going.
Only you decide how you get there.
-Vincent Ivan Phipps

The spiritual life does not remove us from the world
but leads us deeper into it.
-Henri J. M. Nouwen

This is the day which the Lord has made.
Let us rejoice and be glad in it.
Psalms 118:24

God is love.
1 John 4:8

Very early in the morning, while it was still dark,
Jesus got up, left the house and went off to a
solitary place, where he prayed.
Mark 1:35

Computer
Computers are useless.
They can only give you answers.
-Pablo Picasso

The good news: Computers allow us to work 100%
faster. The bad news: They generate 300% more work.
-Unknown

Cooking

The torch of love is lit in the kitchen

No matter where I serve my guests,
they seem to like my kitchen best.

Cooking is like love...
It should be entered into with abandon or not at all.
-Harriet Van Horne

Only the pure of heart can make good soup.
-Beethoven

Crafts

When life gives you scraps, make something with them.

Crafting fills my days
-not to mention the living room, bedroom and closets!

My husband lets me have
all the craft supplies I can hide!

A family stitched together with love...seldom unravels.

One craft project, like one cookie, is never enough!

There is a time to be born and a time to die,
A time to laugh and a time to cry,
But there never seems to be enough time to sew!

Blessed are the children of the piecemakers . . .
for they shall inherit the quilts!

Hands to work, hearts to God.
-Shaker saying

Happiness lies in the joy of achievement and the thrill of creative effort.
-Franklin Roosevelt

We're all only fragile threads, but what a tapestry we make.
-Jerry Ellis

Crawling
Oh, the places you'll go!
-Dr. Seuss

By perseverance the snail reached the ark.
-Charles Haddon Spurgeon

Crying
Only eyes washed by tears can see clearly.
-Louis L. Mann

Tears are the summer showers to the soul.
-Alfred Austin

The soul would have no rainbow had the eyes no tears.
-John Vance Cheney

Tears fall from heaven and a frown of darkness settles overhead.
-K B Ballentine

Dance

Dance like no one's watching.

Dance to the song of life.
-Katherine Hepburn

Let your life lightly dance
on the edges of time
like dew on the tip of a leaf.
-Rabindranath Tagore

Nobody cares if you can't dance well.
Just get up and dance.
-Dave Barry

Dancing is the loftiest, the most moving,
the most beautiful of the arts, because it is no mere
translation or abstraction from life; it is life itself.
-Havelock Ellis

The body says what words cannot.
-Martha Graham

Dancing is the body made poetic.
-Ernst Bacon

If you can walk, you can dance.
-Zimbabwe saying

Music is well said to be the speech of angels.
-Thomas Carlyle

Daughter
(see also Baby, Child, and Girl)

Always my daughter, now my friend.

*Daughters are little girls that grow up
to be your best friend.*

*A daughter can light up your day just
by blinking her big, bright eyes.*
-Crystal Dawn Perry

Death (special memories)
To live in hearts we leave behind is not to die.
-Thomas Campbell

*We call that person who has lost his father, an orphan;
and a widower that man who has lost his wife.
But that man who has known the immense unhappiness of
losing a friend, by what name do we call him? Here every
language is silent
and holds its peace in impotence.*
-Joseph Roux

*The bitterest tears shed over graves are for
words left unsaid and deeds left undone.*
-Harriet Beecher Stowe

It matters not how a man dies, but how he lives.
-Samuel Johnson

*Even though I walk through the valley of the shadow
of death, I will fear no evil, for you are with me;
your rod and staff, they comfort me.*
Psalms 23:4

Precious in the sight of the Lord is the death of his saints.
Psalm 116:15

138

Diet

Friendships come in many sizes
and ours is Extra-Large.

I've been on a constant diet for the last two decades.
I've lost a total of 789 pounds. By all accounts,
I should be hanging from a charm bracelet.

-Erma Bombeck

Life is like a box of chocolates.

-Forrest Gump

Dog

Don't accept your dog's admiration as
conclusive evidence that you are wonderful.

-Ann Landers

Dogs are not our whole life,
but they make our life whole.

-Roger Caras

Hang around doggies and kids; they know how to play.

-Geoffrey Godbey

The dog is the god of frolic.

-Henry Ward Beecher

A dog wags its tail with its heart.

-Martin Buxbaum

No matter how little money
and how few possessions you own,
having a dog makes you rich.

-Louis Sabin

Do-it-yourself

If you build it, they will come.

*The ark was built by amateurs
and the Titanic by experts.
Don't wait for experts.*

-Murray Cohen

Doll

*The little girl expects no declaration of tenderness
from her doll. She loves it, and that's all.
It is thus that we should love.*

-De Gourmont

*A girl is ...
Innocence playing in the mud,
Beauty standing on its head, and
Motherhood dragging a doll by the foot.*

-Allan Beck

Dreams

Conceive it. Believe it. Achieve it.

Dreams are the touchstones of our character.

-Henry David Thoreau

*Go confidently in the direction of your dreams.
Live the life you've imagined.*

-Henry David Thoreau

*A dream is a wish your heart makes
when you're fast asleep.*

-Cinderella

*The future belongs to those
who believe in the beauty of their dreams.*
-E. Roosevelt

*My eyes are an ocean
in which my dreams are reflected.*
-Anna Uhlich

Follow your bliss.
-Joseph Campbell

*A dream is in the mind of the believer
and in the hands of the doer.
You are not given a dream
without being given the power to make it come true.*
-Unknown

Hitch your wagon to a star.
-Ralph Waldo Emerson

Yesterday is a dream, tomorrow but a vision.
-Sanskrit Proverb

Everything starts as somebody's daydream.
-Larry Niven

*Children love to be alone because alone is where
they know themselves, and where they dream.*
-Roger Rosenblatt

*All our dreams can come true,
if we have the courage to pursue them.*
-Walt Disney

Will you be the rock that redirects the river?
-Claire Nuer

Make the most of yourself for that is all there is of you.
-Ralph Waldo Emerson

For I know the plans I have for you,
plans to prosper you, to give you hope and a future.
Jeremiah 29:11

Dress-up
You can grow up to be anything you want to be.

The difference between
ordinary and extraordinary
is that little extra.
-John Ruskin

Easter
The Lord has risen indeed!
St. Luke 24:34

Because I live, you shall live also.
John 14:19

This is the day the Lord has made.
Let us rejoice and be glad in it.
Psalms 118:24

Eating
Too much of a good thing is wonderful.
-Mae West

Never eat more than you can lift.
-Miss Piggy

A mother finds out what is meant by "spitting image"
when she tries to feed cereal to her baby.
-Imogene Fay

Exercise

To exercise is human; not to is divine.

-Robert Orben

Fall

It is this time of year that reminds me that another season has gone and yet my life is passing by like a leaf from an oak tree on a windy afternoon; colorful but short lived.

-Jo Stack

*Crunching, crinkling autumn leaves
Spiraling, swirling in the breeze*

-Julie Perkins Cantrell

*Earth is here so kind,
that tickle her with a hoe
and she laughs with a harvest.*

-Douglas Jerrold

*An open home, an open heart...
here grows a bountiful harvest.*

-Judy Hand

*Beauty seen is never lost;
God's colors all are fast.*

-John Greenleaf Whittier

Family

A family stitched together with love...seldom unravels.

Family...another word for love.

A happy family is heaven on earth.

Every family tree always produces nuts.

Family faces are magic mirrors.
Looking at people who belong to us,
we see the past, present and future.
-Gail Lumet Buckley

Other things change us,
but we start and end with the family.
-Anthony Brandt

The family is one of nature's masterpieces.
-George Santayana

A happy family is but an earlier heaven.
-John Bowring

The bond that links your true family is not one of blood,
but of respect and joy in each other's life.
-Richard Bach

The family you come from isn't as
important as the family
you're going to have.
-Ring Lardner

He that raises a large family does,
indeed, while he lives to observe them,
stand a broader mark for sorrow;
but then he stands a broader mark
for pleasure too.
-Benjamin Franklin

Perhaps the greatest social service that can
be rendered by anybody to the country and
to mankind is to bring up a family.
-George Bernard Shaw

The family is the school of duties,
founded on love.

-Felix Adler

Jesus' blood bought us more than salvation
-it bought us a family.

1 Corinthians 10: 16-17

Family Tree

To forget one's ancestors is to be
a brook without a source,
a tree without a root.

-Chinese proverb

Father
(see also Men)

No matter how tall I grow,
I will always look up to my Dad.

I look just like my Daddy.
I have his double chin and a pot belly.

I'm as lucky as can be,
for the world's best dad belongs to me.

The greatest gift I ever had,
it came from God,
I call him Dad.

Anyone can be a Father,
but it takes someone special to be a Daddy.

Hop on Pop. We like to hop. We like to hop on Pop!

-Dr. Seuss

One father is more than a hundred schoolmasters.
-English proverb

*Perhaps the greatest social service that can
be rendered by anybody to the country and
to mankind is to bring up a family.*
-George Bernard Shaw

*The moon was never so close
as when I rode on your shoulders.*
-Unknown

*Fatherhood is pretending the present
you love most is soap-on-a-rope.*
-Bill Cosby

It is much easier to become a father than to be one.
-Kent Nerburn

*Children have never been very good at listening to
their elders, but they have never failed to imitate them.*
-James Baldwin

*Of all nature's gifts to the human race,
what is sweeter to a man than his children?*
-Marcus Tullius Cicero

*One hundred years from now, it will not matter what
my bank account was, how big my house was, or what
kind of car I drove. But the world may be a little
better, because I was important in the life of a child.*
-Forest Witcraft

*What do I owe my father?
Everything.*
-Henry Van Dyke

*The night you were born, I ceased being
my father's boy and became my son's father.
That night I began a new life.*
-Henry Gregor Felson

Safe, for a child, is his father's hand, holding him tight.
-Pam Brown

A father sees himself in his child's eyes.
-Alexander Wood

*The most important thing a father can do for
his children is to love their mother.*
-Henry Ward Beecher

*We never know the love of our parents for us until we
become parents. When we first bend over the cradle of
our own child, God throws back the temple door, and
reveals to us the sacredness and mystery of a father's
and a mother's love to ourselves.*
-Henry Ward Beecher

A child had every toy his father wanted.
-Robert E. Whitten

The glory of children is their father.
Proverbs 17:6

Fear
The only thing we have to fear is fear itself.
-Franklin D. Roosevelt

*Love is what we were born with.
Fear is what we learned here.*
-Marianne Williamson

*The bravest person is not
always the one standing in silence.
The bravest is the person who admits fear,
after they have stepped.*
-Vincent Ivan Phipps

Feel the fear, and do it anyway.
-Susan Jeffers

Fishing
*Fishing for a dream, Fishing near and far,
His line a silver moonbeam, His bait a silver star.*
-Alice C.D. Riley

*Give a man a fish and he had food for a day;
Teach him how to fish
and you can get rid of him for the entire weekend.*
-Zenna Schaffer

Flowers/Gardening
*One is closer to God in a garden
than in anyplace on earth.*

If friends were flowers, I'd pick you.

Flowers are words which even a baby can understand.
-Arthur C. Coxe

Every flower is a soul blossoming out to nature.
-Gerard de Nerval

*Don't judge each day by the harvest you reap,
but by the seeds you plant.*
-Robert Louis Stevenson

*Find the seed at the bottom of your heart
and bring forth a flower.*
-Shigenori Kaneoka

Gardening is an instrument of grace.
-May Sarton

*All gardeners live in beautiful places
because they make them so.*
-Joseph Joubert

*A single rose can be my garden
... a single friend, my world.*
-Leo Buscaglia

The "Amen!" of nature is always a flower.
-Oliver Wendell Holmes, Sr.

*If we could see the miracle of a single flower clearly,
our whole life would change.*
-Buddha

*One of the most tragic things I know about
human nature is that all of us tend to put off living.
We are all dreaming of some magical rose garden over the
horizon - instead of enjoying the roses
blooming outside our windows today.*
-Dale Carnegie

*You can complain because roses have thorns,
or you can rejoice because thorns have roses.*
-Ziggy

*Life is like a flower...
it grows more beautiful the more you care for it.*
-K.C. Rogers

Don't hurry. Don't worry.
You're only here for a short visit.
So be sure to stop and smell the flowers.
-Walter Hagen

Earth is here so kind,
that tickle her with a hoe
and she laughs with a harvest.
-Douglas Jerrold

God gave us our memories so that
we might have roses in December.
-J. M Barrie

Football
(see also Sports)
Football is like life; it requires perseverance,
self-denial, hard work sacrifice, dedication
and respect for authority.
-Vince Lombardi

Most football teams are temperamental.
That's 90% temper and 10% mental.
-Doug Plank

Friendship
Friendship is a blessing.

Side by side or far apart,
true friends live within our heart.

A friend is a gift you give yourself.

To the world you might be one person,
but to one person you might be the world.

To a friend's house the road is never long.

Friends are flowers in the garden of life.

*A friend is someone you can do
nothing with and enjoy it .*

Old friends make the best antiques.

*True friendship is seen through the heart,
not through the eyes.*

*Friendships come in many sizes
and ours is Extra-Large.*

Ever the best of friends.
-Charles Dickens

*Too often we underestimate the power of a touch,
a smile, a kind word, a listening ear,
an honest compliment, or the smallest act of caring:
all of which have the potential to turn a life around.*
-Leo Buscaglia

*Many people will walk in and out of your life.
But only true friends will leave footprints in your heart.*
-Eleanor Roosevelt

*The heart recognizes a true and trusted friend...
it's no wonder my heart knows you so well.*
-Mary Chandler Huff

I am wealthy in my friends.
-William Shakespeare

A true friend is the best possession.
-Benjamin Franklin

What a great blessing is a friend with a heart so trusty,
you may safely bury all your secrets in it.
-Seneca

The best and most beautiful things
in the world cannot be seen or even touched;
they must be felt with the heart.
-Helen Keller

Love is a friendship set to music.
-E. Joseph Cossman

Hold a true friend with both your hands.
-Nigerian proverb

A friend is a person with whom you dare to be yourself.
-Pam Brown

A friend is...
a whole lot of wonderful people rolled into one.
-Gayle Lawrence

It is one of the blessings of friends
is that you can afford to be stupid with them.
-Ralph Waldo Emerson

Don't walk in front of me. I may not follow.
Don't walk behind me. I may not lead.
Walk beside me and be my friend.
-Albert Camus

If you want an accounting of your worth,
count your friends.
-Merry Browne

A friend is one who knows you
and loves you just the same.
-Elbert Hubbard

The real test of friendship is:
Can you literally do nothing with the other person?
Can you enjoy those moments of life
that are utterly simple?
-Eugene Kennedy

A single rose can be my garden...
a single friend, my world.
-Leo Buscaglia

Our friendship brings sunshine to shade,
and shade to sunshine.
-Thomas Burke

A friend may well be reckoned
the masterpiece of Nature.
-Ralph Waldo Emerson

Each friend represents a world in us,
a world possible not born until they arrive,
and it is only by this meeting that a new world is born.
-Anais Nin

We are each of us angels with only one wing,
and we can only fly by embracing one another.
-Luciano de Crescenzo

A friend loves at all times.
Proverbs 17:17

A faithful friend is the medicine of Life.
Ecclesiastes 6:16

Gift

A friend is a gift you give yourself.

*The real secret of happiness is not what you
give or receive; it's what you share.*

*Each day comes bearing it's own gifts.
Untie the ribbons.*

-Ruth Ann Schubacker

Girl/Girls

*Sugar and spice and everything nice,
that's what little girls are made of.*

Little girls are the nicest things that happen to people.

-Allan Beck

*A girl is ...
Innocence playing in the mud,
Beauty standing on its head, and
Motherhood dragging a doll by the foot.*

-Allan Beck

*The little girl expects no declaration of tenderness
from her doll. She loves it, and that's all.
It is thus that we should love.*

-De Gourmont

*She has the spirit of the sun,
The moods of the moon,
The will of the wind.*

-Julie Perkins Cantrell

Golf
Live...Laugh...GOLF!!!
-Kathryn Schaefer Plaum

Golf is a good walk spoiled.
-Mark Twain

Golf is the cruelest game, because eventually it will drag you out in front of the whole school, take your lunch money and slap you around.
-Rick Reilly

Graduation
There are no shortcuts to life's greatest achievements.

You can grow up to be anything you want to be.

It's never too late to be the person you might have been.
-George Eliot

Dreams are the touchstones of our character.
-Henry David Thoreau

Go confidently in the direction of your dreams. Live the life you've imagined.
-Henry David Thoreau

The future belongs to those who believe in the beauty of their dreams.
-Eleanor Roosevelt

Training is everything. The peach was once a bitter almond; cauliflower is nothing but cabbage with a college education.
-Mark Twain

Grandchildren

Grandchildren are the gifts of yesterday,
the pride of today and the joy of tomorrow.

Grandparents are made in heaven,
born with the birth of
their first grandchild.

Grandchildren are God's way of
compensating us for growing old.
-Mary H. Waldrip

Grandparents somehow sprinkle a sense
of stardust over grandchildren.
-Alex Haley

When a child is born, so is a grandmother.
-Italian proverb

Never have children, only grandchildren.
-Gore Vidal

One of the most powerful handclasps is that of a new
grandbaby around the finger of a grandfather.
-Joy Hargrove

Children have never been very good at listening to
their elders, but they have never failed to imitate them.
-James Baldwin

It is one of nature's ways that we often feel
closer to distant generations than to the
generations immediately preceding us.
-Igor Stravinsky

The best games between children and grandfathers are timeless, and there seems to be nothing better to bridge the generation gap than play.

-Vincent MacKenzie

Getting to know the youngest people in my life has been a joy.

-Frank Tarloff

The soul is healed by being with children.

-Fyodor Dostoevsky

What makes a boy more brilliant than being a grandson?

-Tom Berg

Where children are, there is the Golden Age.

-Novalis

Children's children are a crown to the aged, and parents are the pride of their children.

Proverbs 17:6

Grandfather
(see also Grandparents)

My greatest blessings call me Poppa.

I look just like my Grandpa. I have his double chin and a pot belly.

The moon was never so close as when I rode on your shoulders.

-Unknown

Grandfathers are gentle but strong;
to children they are like a port in a storm,
warm and secure.
-Joan Bartlett

From the days of the first grandfather,
everyone has remembered a golden age behind him.
-James Russell Lowell

Grandfathers impart information, ethics, and values
that children learn nowhere else.
-Arthur Kornhaber

The best games between children and grandfathers
are timeless, and there seems to be nothing better
to bridge the generation gap than play.
-Vincent MacKenzie

Every grandfather believes in heredity until his
grandchildren start making fools of themselves.
-Simon Schwartz

You've got to do your own growing,
no matter how tall your grandfather was.
-Irish proverb

One of the most powerful handclasps is that of a new
grandbaby around the finger of a grandfather.
-Joy Hargrove

That the aged men be sober, grave, temperate,
sound in faith, in charity, in patience.
Titus 2:2

Grandmother
(see also Grandparents)

My greatest blessings call me Grandmommie.

Grandmothers are angels in disguise.

*Sunshine is to flowers what a
Grandmother is to her grandchildren.*

The road to Grandma's house is never long.

Grandmas are antique little girls.

*Over the river and through the woods,
to Grandmother's house we go...*

A grandmother is a mother who has a second chance.

*A grandmother is a special blend
Of sweetness, care and love without end.*

When a child is born, so is a grandmother.
-Italian proverb

*If your baby is "beautiful and perfect, never
cries or fusses, sleeps on schedule and burps
on demand, an angel all the time,"
you're the grandma.*
-Theresa Bloomingdale

*The aged women likewise, that they be in
behaviour as becometh holiness, not false
accusers, not given to much wine,
teachers of good things.*
Titus 2:3

Grandparents

Grandparents are made in heaven, born
with the birth of their first grandchild.

For love lavished beyond all measure
For happy hours to always treasure...
I love my grandparents
with all my heart.

Family faces are magic mirrors.
Looking at people who belong to us,
we see the past, present and future.
-Gail Lumet Buckley

Grandparents, like heroes, are as
necessary to a child's growth as vitamins.
-Joyce Allston

Old love rusts not.
-German proverb

Life is no brief candle to me.
It is a sort of splendid torch which I've got
hold of for the moment and I want to make
it burn as brightly as possible before
handing it on to the future generations.
-George Bernard Shaw

Grandparents somehow sprinkle a sense
of stardust over grandchildren.
-Alex Haley

Age shall not weary them, nor the years condemn.
-Laurence Binyon

It is one of nature's ways that we often feel
closer to distant generations than to the
generations immediately preceding us.
-Igor Stravinsky

Children have never been very good at listening to
their elders, but they have never failed to imitate them.
-James Baldwin

One hundred years from now, it will not matter what
my bank account was, how big my house was, or what
kind of car I drove. But the world may be a little
better, because I was important in the life of a child.
-Forest Witcraft

When grandparents enter the door,
discipline flies out the window.
-Ogden Nash

Getting to know the youngest people
in my life has been a joy.
-Frank Tarloff

The simplest toy, one which even the youngest child
can operate, is called a grandparent.
-Sam Levenson

If wrinkles must be written upon our brows,
let them not be written upon the heart.
The spirit should not grow old.
-James A. Garfield

Few things are more delightful than
grandchildren fighting over your lap.
-Doug Larson

*If I had known how wonderful
it would be to have grandchildren,
I'd have had them first.*

-Lois Wyse

Growing up

*No matter how tall I grow,
I will always look up to my Dad.*

*There is always one moment in childhood
when the door opens and lets the future in.*

-Graham Greene

*Not a having and a resting,
but a growing and a becoming.*

-Matthew Arnold

*Surprisingly lively, precious days.
What is there to say except: here they are.
Sifting through my fingers like sand.*

-Joyce Carol Oates

*You've got to do your own growing,
no matter how tall your grandfather was.*

-Irish proverb

Halloween

'Tis now the very witching time of night.

-William Shakespeare

*Double, double toil and trouble;
Fire burn and cauldron bubble.*

-William Shakespeare

Handicap

I have never been disabled in my dreams.
-Christopher Reeves

*One of the things I learned the hard way was that it
doesn't pay to get discouraged.
Keeping busy and making optimism a way of life
can restore your faith in yourself.*
-Lucille Ball

*We learn as much from sorrow as from joy,
as much from illness as from health,
from handicap as from advantage
-and indeed perhaps more.*
-Pearl S. Buck

*I seldom think about my limitations,
and they never make me sad.
Perhaps there is just a touch of yearning at times;
but it is vague, like a breeze among flowers.*
-Helen Keller

Happiness

There is only one happiness in life, to love and be loved.
-George Sands

*The real secret of happiness is not what you
give or receive; it's what you share.*
-Unknown

*The grand essentials to happiness in this life
are something to do, something to love
and something to hope for.*
-Joseph Addison

Sunshine on my shoulders makes me happy.
-John Denver

Your own sky will lighten, if other skies you brighten
by just being happy with a heart full of song.
-Ripley D. Saunders

Too much of a good thing is wonderful.
-Mae West

If you're too busy to enjoy life, you're too busy.
-Jeff Davidson

He is happiest, be he king or peasant,
who finds peace in his home.
-Johann von Goethe

Happiness is a butterfly, which, when pursued,
is always just beyond your grasp, but which,
if you will sit down quietly, may alight upon you.
-Nathaniel Hawthorne

Love is the master key,
which opens the gates of happiness.
-Oliver Wendell Holmes, Sr.

Hardship/Illness/Injury
I am not afraid of storms,
for I am learning how to sail my ship.
-Louisa May Alcott

God grant me the Serenity
to accept the things I cannot change;
Courage to change the things I can;
and Wisdom to know the difference.
-Anonymous Prayer

In three words I can sum up everything
I've learned about life...
It goes on.
-Robert Frost

So never let a cloudy day ruin your sunshine,
for even if you can't see it,
the sunshine is still there,
inside of you ready to shine
when you will let it.
-Amy Pitzele

Heartbreak is life educating us.
-George Bernard Shaw

Life is not the way it's supposed to be.
It's the way it is.
The way you cope with it is
what makes the difference.
-Virginia Satir

There are days when you don't
have a song in your heart.
Sing anyway.
-Emory Austin

All the world is full of suffering.
It is also full of overcoming it.
-Helen Keller

We learn as much from sorrow as from joy,
as much from illness as from health,
from handicap as from advantage
-and indeed perhaps more.
-Pearl S. Buck

I don't think of all the misery
but the beauty that still remains.

-Anne Frank

When things are bad, we take comfort in the thought
that they could always be worse.
And when they are, we find hope in the thought that
things are so bad they have to get better.

-Malcolm Forbes

Repeat to yourself the most comforting words of all:
This, too, shall pass.

-Ann Landers

Pain is important;
How we evade it, how we succumb to it,
How we deal with it, how we transcend it.

-Audre Lorde

A cheerful heart is good medicine,
but a crushed spirit dries up the bones.

Proverbs 17:22

A faithful friend is the medicine of Life.

Ecclesiastes 6:16

My flesh and my heart may fail,
but God is the strength of my heart
and my portion forever.

Psalm 73:26

Heart

*A mother's heart is a special place
where children can always go home.*

*I carry your heart with me;
I carry it in my heart.*
-E. E. Cummings

*The best and most beautiful things in the world
cannot be seen or even touched;
they must be felt with the heart.*
-Helen Keller

*The heart hath its own memory, like the mind,
and in it are enshrined the precious keepsakes.*
-Unknown

*It's only with the heart that one can see clearly;
what's essential is invisible to the eye.*
-Lerner & Lowe

*Write in your heart that everyday
is the best day of the year.*
-Ralph Waldo Emerson

*What a great blessing is a friend with a heart so trusty
you may safely bury all your secrets in it.*
-Seneca

*The heart recognizes a true and trusted friend...
it's no wonder my heart knows you so well.*
-Mary Chandler Huff

The heart sees better than the eye.
-Hebrew Proverb

*Many people will walk in and out of your life
but only a true friend will leave footprints in your heart.*
-Eleanor Roosevelt

*Find the seed at the bottom of your heart
and bring forth a flower.*
-Shigenori Kaneoka

*Two souls but with a single thought
-two hearts that beat as one.*
-Maria Lovell

Hands to work, hearts to God.
-Shaker saying

The mother's heart is the child's schoolroom.
-Henry Ward Beecher

*There are days when you don't
have a song in your heart.
Sing anyway.*
-Emory Austin

*For where your treasure is,
there will your heart be also.*
Matthew 6:21

A happy heart makes the face cheerful.
Proverbs 15:13

Blessed are the pure in heart, for they shall see God.
Matthew 5:8

Hockey
(see also Sports)

You miss 100% of the shots you don't take.
-Wayne Gretzky

*We take the shortest route to the puck
and arrive in ill humor.*
-Bobby Clarke

Home/House

*Houses are made of wood and stone,
but only love can make a home.*

*No matter where I serve my guests,
they seem to like my kitchen best.*

*God bless America,
my home sweet home.*
-Irving Berlin

Be it ever so humble, there's no place like home.
-J.H. Payne

*He is happiest, be he king or peasant,
who finds peace in his home.*
-Johann von Goethe

*Mi casa es tu casa
(My house is your house)*
Spanish or English

*...there was still room to turn around in,
but not to swing a cat in,
at least not with entire security to the cat.*
-Mark Twain

Home is an invention on which no one has yet improved.
-Ann Douglas

One hundred years from now, it will not matter what my bank account was, how big my house was, or what kind of car I drove. But the world may be a little better, because I was important in the life of a child.
-Forest Witcraft

An open home, an open heart, here grows a bountiful harvest.
-Judy Hand

Unless the Lord builds the house, it's builders labor in vain.
Psalm 127:1

Home School
(see also School)
The family is the school of duties, founded on love.
-Felix Adler

For the mother is and must be, whether she knows it or not, the greatest, strongest and most lasting teacher her children have.
-Hannah Whitall Smith

The mother's heart is the child's schoolroom.
-Henry Ward Beecher

One good mother is worth a hundred schoolmasters.
-George Herbert

The home is the chief school of human virtues.
-William Ellery Channing

Horse

Horses make a landscape look beautiful.
-Alice Walker

Horses are predictably unpredictable.
-Loretta Gage

They are more beautiful than anything in the world,
kinetic sculptures, perfect form in motion.
-Kate Millett

Sit loosely in the saddle of life.
-Robert Louis Stevenson

Hug

Hold a true friend with both your hands.
-Nigerian proverb

The love we give away is the only love we keep.
-Elbert Hubbard

To love and to be loved
is to feel the sun from both sides.
-David Viscott

Love comforteth like sunshine after rain.
-William Shakespeare

A hug is a roundabout way of expressing emotion.
-Gideon Wurdz

Too often we underestimate the power of a touch,
a smile, a kind word, a listening ear,
an honest compliment, or the smallest act of caring:
all of which have the potential to turn a life around.
-Leo Buscaglia

Inspirational
God grant me the Serenity
to accept the things I cannot change;
Courage to change the things I can;
and Wisdom to know the difference.
-Anonymous prayer

When you reach the end of your rope,
tie a knot in it and hang on.
-Thomas Jefferson

You can complain because roses have thorns,
or you can rejoice because thorns have roses.
-Ziggy

Kiss
The love we give away is the only love we keep.
-Elbert Hubbard

A lawful kiss is never worth a stolen one.
-Maupassant

Kite
Imagination is the highest kite one can fly.
-Lauren Bacall

Laugh
We cannot really love anybody
with whom we never laugh.
-Agnes Repplier

Laugh, and the world laughs with you.
-Ella Wheeler Wilcox

A smile is a whisper of a laugh.
-A child's definition

"When the first baby laughed for the first time, the laugh broke into thousands of pieces and they all went skipping about, and that was the beginning of fairies."
(from Peter Pan)

Blessed is he who has learned to laugh at himself, for he shall never cease to be entertained.
-John Powell

Laughter is the sun that drives winter from the human face.
-Victor Hugo

The joy of the heart makes the face merry.
-English Proverb

The child in you, like all children, loves to laugh, to be around people who can laugh at themselves and life. Children instinctively know that the more laughter we have in our lives, the better.
-Wayne Dyer

Laughter is the most healthful exertion.
-Christoph Wilhelm Hufeland

Life
It's a very short trip. While alive, live.
-Malcolm Forbes

In three words I can sum up everything I've learned about life... It goes on.
-Robert Frost

Life isn't a matter of milestones, but of moments.
-Rose Kennedy

Each day comes bearing it's own gifts.
Untie the ribbons.
-Ruth Ann Schubacker

Normal day,
let me be aware
of the treasure that you are.
-Mary Jean Irion

I am beginning to learn that it is the
sweet, simple things of life
which are the real ones after all.
-Laura Ingalls Wilder

Life is like a box of chocolates.
-Forrest Gump

Life is a great big canvas;
throw all the paint on it you can.
-Danny Kaye

For all of us,
today's experiences
are tomorrow's memories.
-Barbara Johnson

Our lives are a mosaic of little things.
-Ingrid Trobisch

Enjoy the little things in life,
for one day you will look back and
realize they were the big things.
-Unknown

Make the most of yourself
for that is all there is of you.
-Ralph Waldo Emerson

Surprisingly lively, precious days.
What is there to say except: here they are.
Sifting through my fingers like sand.
-Joyce Carol Oates

If you ask me what I came into this world
to do, I will tell you: I came to live out loud.
-Emile Zola

I think of life itself, now,
as a wonderful play that I've written for myself...
and so my purpose is to have
the most fun playing my part.
-Shirley MacLaine

Life is not the way it's supposed to be.
It's the way it is.
The way you cope with it is
what makes the difference.
-Virginia Satir

Be yourself! Who else is better qualified?
-Frank J. Giblin

I thank you God for this most amazing day;
for the leaping greenly spirits of trees
and a blue true dream of sky;
and for everything which is natural,
which is infinite, which is yes.
-E.E. Cummings

Let your life lightly dance
on the edges of time like
dew on the tip of a leaf.
-Rabindranath Tagore

The purpose of life is a life of purpose.
-Robert Byrne

The only way to live is to accept
each minute as an unrepeatable miracle,
which is exactly what it is:
a miracle and unrepeatable.
-Storm Jameson

Life is like a flower...
it grows more beautiful the more you care for it.
-K.C. Rogers

Every day in a life fills the whole life
with expectation and memory.
-C.S. Lewis

Measure wealth not by the things you have,
but by the things you have for which
you would not take any money.
-Unknown

That man is a success who has
lived well, laughed often and loved much.
-Robert Louis Stevenson

If you're too busy to enjoy life, you're too busy.
-Jeff Davidson

That it will never come again is what makes life so sweet.
-Emily Dickinson

Be glad of life because it gives you the
chance to love, and to work, and to play
and to look up at the stars.

-Henry Van Dyke

Write in your heart that everyday
is the best day of the year.

-Ralph Waldo Emerson

One of the most tragic things I know about human
nature is that all of us tend to put off living.
We are all dreaming of some magical rose garden
over the horizon – instead of enjoying the roses
blooming outside our windows today.

-Dale Carnegie

Don't hurry. Don't worry.
You're only here for a short visit.
So be sure to stop and smell the flowers.

-Walter Hagen

Live each day as you would climb a mountain…
Climb slowly, steadily; enjoying each passing moment;
and the view from the summit will serve
as a fitting climax for the journey.

-Harold V. Melchert

We're all only fragile threads,
but what a tapestry we make.

-Jerry Ellis

It's not the years in your life
but the life in your years that counts.

-Adlai Stevenson

Live your life and forget your age.
-Frank Bering

A faithful friend is the medicine of life.
Ecclesiastes 6:16

This is the day which the Lord has made.
Let us rejoice and be glad in it.
Psalms 118:24

Love
Love bears all things,
Believes all things,
Hopes all things,
Endures all things,
Love never fails.

Live well, Laugh often, Love much.

Love is a smile that grows from year to year.

A Sister is a special gift of Love.

Draw a circle, not a heart, around the one you love
because a heart can break but a circle goes on forever.

Love is above all the gift of oneself.
-Jean Anouilh

We cannot really love anybody
with whom we never laugh.
-Agnes Repplier

You brighten my life through storm and rain
Like a million stars shining...forever
-Najah T. Clemmons

Where there is great love,
there are miracles.
-Willa Cather

To love and to be loved
is to feel the sun from both sides.
-David Viscott

I carry your heart with me;
I carry it in my heart.
-E. E. Cummings

Love comforteth like sunshine after rain.
-William Shakespeare

Yours is the light by which my spirit's born.
-E. E. Cummings

Love is a many splendored thing.
-Paul Francis Webster

Love is heaven, and heaven is love!
-Sir Walter Scott

Love is all you need.
-the Beatles

There is only one happiness in life, to love and be loved.
-George Sands

Two souls but with a single thought
-two hearts that beat as one.
-Maria Lovell

Love is the discovery of ourselves in others,
and the delight in the recognition.
-Alexander Smith

Sometimes love is for a moment.
Sometimes love is for a lifetime.
Sometimes a moment is a lifetime.
-Unknown

The grand essentials to happiness in this life are
something to do, something to love
and something to hope for.
-Joseph Addison

Love is the master key,
which opens the gates of happiness.
-Oliver Wendell Holmes, Sr.

Love is a friendship set to music.
-E. Joseph Cossman

You can't think how I depend on you,
and when you're not there,
the color goes out of my life.
-Virginia Woolf

Old love rusts not.
-German proverb

The love we give away is the only love we keep.
-Elbert Hubbard

The most precious possession that ever
comes to a man in this world
is a woman's heart.
-Josiah G. Holland

True lovers live in a world of fools.
-Vincent Ivan Phipps

Love is what we were born with.
Fear is what we learned here.
-Marianne Williamson

Ultimately, love is everything.
-M. Scott Peck

No one has ever seen God;
but if we love one another,
God lives in us and his
love is made complete in us.
1 John 4:12

Mercy, peace and love be
yours in abundance.
Jude 2

Make-Believe
We have only to believe.
-Pierre Teilhard de Chardin

"When the first baby laughed for the first time,
the laugh broke into thousands of pieces
and they all went skipping about,
and that was the beginning of fairies."
(from Peter Pan)

Why, sometimes, I've believed as many
as six impossible things before breakfast.
-Lewis Carroll, Through the Looking Glass

Memories

The heart hath its own memory, like the mind,
and in it are enshrined the precious keepsakes.

What was hard to endure is sweet to recall.

We do not remember days. We remember moments.
-Cesare Pavese

Recall it as often as you wish;
a happy memory never wears out.
-Libbie Fudim

God gave us our memories so that
we might have roses in December.
-J. M Barrie

Every day in a life fills the whole life
with expectation and memory.
-C.S. Lewis

Fond memory brings the light of other days around me.
-Thomas Moore

Some memories are realities, and are better than
anything that can ever happen to one again.
-Willa Cather

Those are the memories that make me a wealthy soul....
-Bob Seger

The past is just the beginning of a beginning.
-H.G. Wells

The stories that you tell about your past, shape your future.
-Eric Ransdell

Men
It's not the men in my life;
it's the life in my men.
-Mae West

The measure of a man is in the lives he's touched.
-Ernie Banks

Life begins as a quest of the child for the man and ends
as a journey by the man to rediscover the child.
-Laurens van der Post

Great is the man who has not lost his childlike heart.
-Mencius

Boys will be boys, and so will a lot of middle-aged men.
-Kin Hubbard

Military
(see also Patriotic)
Ask not what your country can do for you,
but what you can do for your country.
-John Fitzgerald Kennedy

I regret that I have but one life to give for my country.
-Nathan Hale

The mothers of brave men must themselves be brave.
-Mary Ball Washington

And the sea will grant each man new hope,
as sleep brings dreams of home.
-Christopher Columbus

Money

Money talks all right. Usually it says, "Good-bye."

Measure wealth not by the things you have,
but by the things you have for which
you would not take any money.
-Unknown

Children are poor men's riches.
-English Proverb

If you want an accounting of your worth,
count your friends.
-Merry Browne

One hundred years from now, it will not matter what
my bank account was, how big my house was, or what
kind of car I drove. But the world may be a little
better, because I was important in the life of a child.
-Forest Witcraft

Do what you love, the money will follow.
-Marsha Sinetar

Diligent hands bring wealth.
Proverbs 10:4

Mother

Home is in my mother's eyes.

Mothers hold their children's hands for awhile,
their hearts forever.

A mother's children are portraits of herself.

Every mother is a working woman.

*A mother's heart is a special place
where children can always go home.*

*God could not be everywhere.
Therefore, he made mothers.*
-Jewish Proverb

The mother's heart is the child's schoolroom.
-Henry Ward Beecher

Motherhood: All love begins and ends there.
-Robert Browning

*A mother's love is an eternal flame,
forever sparked by her children's own.*
-Suzanne Smith

*Who takes the child by hand,
takes the mother by the heart.*
-Danish proverb

*A mother is she who can take the place of all others
but whose place no one else can take.*
-Cardinal Mermillod

*For the mother is and must be,
whether she knows it or not, the greatest, strongest
and most lasting teacher her children have.*
-Hannah Whitall Smith

The purpose of life is a life of purpose.
-Robert Byrne

*Mother is the name for God
in the lips and hearts of children.*
-William Makepeace Thacheray

There is no place I'd rather be tonight,
except in my mother's arms.
-Duke Ellington

Dear Mother,
You know that nothing can ever change
what we have always been
and always will be to each other.
-Franklin Roosevelt

When you have a good mother and no father,
God kind of sits in. It's not enough, but it helps.
-Dick Gregory

We never know the love of our parents for us until we
become parents. When we first bend over the cradle of
our own child, God throws back the temple door, and
reveals to us the sacredness and mystery of a father's
and a mother's love to ourselves.
-Henry Ward Beecher

What a privilege it is to treasure your mother.
-Katie Couric

There is no other closeness in human life like
the closeness between a mother and her baby:
chronologically, physically, and spiritually,
they are just a few heartbeats away
from being the same person.
-Susan Cheever

My mother had a great deal of trouble with me,
but I think she enjoyed it.
-Mark Twain

A mother fills a place so great that there isn't an angel in heaven who wouldn't be glad to give a bushel of diamonds to come down here and take her place.
-Billy Sunday

Nothing else will ever make you as happy or as sad, as proud or as tired, as motherhood.
-Elia Parsons

If evolution really works, how come mothers only have two hands?
-Milton Berle

All that I am or hope to be, I owe to my mother.
-Abraham Lincoln

No language can express the power and beauty and heroism and majesty of a mother's love.
-E. H Chapin

No song or poem will bear my mother's name, yet, so many stories that I write, that we all write, are my mother's stories.
-Alice Walker

There is a harmony and beauty in the life of mother and son that brims the mind's cup of satisfaction.
-Christopher Morley

There is a religion in all deep love, but the love of a mother is the veil of a softer light between the heart and the heavenly Father.
-Samuel Taylor Coleridge

Her children arise up, and call her blessed.
Proverbs 31:28

Music

If you don't toot your own horn,
no one will hear your music.
-Robert B. Barkelew

Music is love in search of a word.
-Sidney Lanier

The woods would be a quiet place
if only the birds that thought
they could sing were singing.
-Unknown

The infant is music itself.
-Hazrat Inayat Khan

Love is a friendship set to music.
-E. Joseph Cossman

Nature

Nature gives to every time and season
some beauties of its own.
-Charles Dickens

A friend may well be reckoned
the masterpiece of Nature.
-Ralph Waldo Emerson

Every flower is a soul blossoming out to nature.
-Gerard de Nerval

Nature is too thin a screen;
the glory of the omnipresent God
bursts through everywhere.
-Ralph Waldo Emerson

I thank you God for this most amazing day;
for the leaping greenly spirits of trees
and a blue true dream of sky;
and for everything which is natural,
which is infinite, which is yes.

-E.E. Cummings

Let your life lightly dance
on the edges of time
like dew on the tip of a leaf.

-Rabindranath Tagore

Though we travel the world over to find the beautiful,
we must carry it with us or we find it not.

-Ralph Waldo Emerson

Live each day as you would climb a mountain...
Climb slowly, steadily; enjoying each passing moment;
and the view from the summit will serve
as a fitting climax for the journey.

-Harold V. Melchert

A brother is a friend given by Nature.

-Legouve

In all things of nature,
there is something of the marvelous.

-Aristotle

The "Amen!" of nature is always a flower.

-Oliver Wendell Holmes, Sr.

Nature always tends to act in the simplest way.

-Bernoulli

Come forth into the light of things;
let nature be your teacher.
-William Wordsworth

Speak to the earth, and it shall teach thee.
Job 12:8

Hurt not the earth, neither the sea, not the trees.
Rev. 7:3

Patriotism
God bless America,
my home sweet home.
-Irving Berlin

Ask not what your country can do for you,
but what you can do for your country.
-John Fitzgerald Kennedy

The union of hearts,
the union of hands,
and the flag of our union forever.
-George Pope Morris

I regret that I have but one life to give for my country.
-Nathan Hale

There is nothing wrong with America that cannot be
cured with what is right in America.
-William J. Clinton

Neighbor
Thou shalt love thy neighbor as thyself.
Romans 13:9

Rain

Tears fall from Heaven and
a frown of darkness settles overhead
-K B Ballentine

Love comforteth like sunshine after rain.
-William Shakespeare

You brighten my life through storm and rain
like a million stars shining...forever.
-Najah T. Clemmons

If you want to see the rainbow,
you have to put up with the rain.
-Dolly Parton

Sunshine is delicious, rain is refreshing,
wind braces us up, snow is exhilarating;
there is really no such thing as bad weather,
only different kinds of good weather.
-John Ruskin

Our friendship brings sunshine to shade,
and shade to sunshine.
-Thomas Burke

For there is no friend like a sister
in calm or stormy weather.
-Christina Rosetti

So never let a cloudy day ruin your sunshine,
for even if you can't see it, the sunshine is still there,
inside of you ready to shine when you will let it.
-Amy Pitzele

Rainbow

The soul would have no rainbow
had the eyes no tears.
-John Vance Cheney

If you want to see the rainbow,
you have to put up with the rain.
-Dolly Parton

My heart leaps up when I behold a rainbow in the sky.
-William Wordsworth

The work will wait while you show the child the rainbow;
but the rainbow won't wait while you do the work.
-Patricia Clafford

I have set my rainbow in the clouds, and it will be
the sign of the covenant between me and the earth.
Genesis 9:13

Retirement

A man is known by the company that keeps him
on after retirement age.

The best time to start thinking about your
retirement is before the boss does.

It's never too late to be the person you might have been.

Don't make a living at the expense of life.

Don't forget until too late that the business of life
is not business, but living.
-B.C. Forbes

Nobody loves life like him who is growing old.
-Sophocles

*Work is what you do so that some time
you won't have to do it anymore.*
-Alfred Polgar

*Men seek out retreats for themselves in the country,
by the seaside, on the mountains...
but all this is unphilosophical to the last degree...
when thou canst at a moment's notice retire into thyself.*
-Marcus Aelius Aurelius

Running
*Even if you're on the right track,
you'll get run over if you just sit there.*
-Will Rogers

*A journey of a thousand miles
must begin with a single step.*
-Chinese proverb

By perseverance the snail reached the ark.
-Charles Haddon Spurgeon

*The distance is nothing.
It's only the first step that's important.*
-Marquise Du Deffand

*Do you not know that in a race all the runners run,
but only one gets the prize?
Run in such a way as to get the prize.*
1 Corinthians 9:24

Let us run with patience the race that is set before us.
Hebrews 12:1

School
(also available: Home school)
What we learn with pleasure we never forget.
-Louis Mercier

Develop a passion for learning.
If you do, you will never cease to grow.
-A.J. D'Anjelo

I have never let my schooling
interfere with my education.
-Mark Twain

Apply your heart to instruction
and your ears to words of knowledge.
Proverbs 23:12

Scrapbooks
(see also Memories)
When life gives you scraps, make a scrapbook.

Scrapbooking fill my days
-Not to mention the living room, bedroom and closets!

My husband lets me have
all the scrapbook supplies I can hide!

One layout, like one cookie, is never enough!

There is a time to be born and a time to die,
A time to laugh and a time to cry,
But there never seems to be enough time to scrapbook!

Blessed are the children of the scrapbookers. . .
for they shall inherit the scrapbooks!

Tell all the stars above,
this is dedicated to the one I love...

Happiness lies in the joy of achievement
and the thrill of creative effort.
-Franklin Roosevelt

More than paper,
Ribbons and string
Are memories of the heart.
-Najah T. Clemmons

To forget one's ancestors is to be
a brook without a source,
a tree without a root.
-Chinese proverb

The beauty of the written word
is that it can be held close to the heart
and read over and over again.
-Florence Littauer

The stories that you tell about your past,
shape your future.
-Eric Ransdell

How will our children know who they are
if they don't know where they came from?
-Ma, Grapes of Wrath

Singing

Always keep a song in your heart.

Sing as if no one can hear you.

To every joyous event comes a chorus of angels.

Dance to the song of life.
-Katherine Hepburn

The woods would be a very silent place
if no birds sang except those that sang best.
-Henry Van Dyke

Hope is the thing with feathers
that perches in the soul
and sings the tune without words
and never stops, at all.
-Emily Dickinson

If you ask me what I came into this world
to do, I will tell you: I came to live out loud.
-Emile Zola

I celebrate myself, and sing myself.
-Walt Whitman

Your own sky will lighten,
if other skies you brighten
by just being happy
with a heart full of song.
-Ripley D. Saunders

There are days when you don't have
a song in your heart.
Sing anyway.
-Emory Austin

Sing and make music in your heart to the Lord,
always giving thanks to God the Father for everything,
in the name of our Lord Jesus Christ.
Ephesians 5:19-20

Sister
A Sister is a special gift of Love.

Forever my Sister, Forever my Friend.

Sisters by birth, best friends by choice.

For there is no friend like a sister
in calm or stormy weather.
-Christina Rosetti

It is because we are different
that each of us is special.
-Brian Dyson

Not many may know the depths of true sisterly love.
-Margaret Courtney

One's sister is a part of one's essential self,
an eternal presence of one's heart and soul and memory.
-Susan Cahill

Those who tease you, love you.
-Jewish proverb

Sleep

A dream is a wish your heart makes
when you're fast asleep.
-Cinderella

Baby's fishing for a dream, Fishing near and far,
His line a silver moonbeam is, His bait a silver star.
-Alice C.D. Riley

In the evening, after she has gone to sleep,
I kneel beside the crib and touch her face,
where it is pressed against the slats, with mine.
-Joan Didion

To sleep, Perchance to Dream.
-William Shakespeare

There is no place I'd rather be tonight,
except in my mother's arms.
-Duke Ellington

People who say they sleep like babies
usually don't have them.
-Leo J. Burke

There never was a child so lovely
but his mother was glad to get him asleep.
-Ralph Waldo Emerson

The future belongs to those who believe
in the beauty of their dreams.
-E. Roosevelt

You can't wake a person
who is pretending to be asleep.
-Navajo proverb

Oh, yes, it's nice to get up in the morning,
but it's nicer to lie in bed.
-Sir Harry Lauder

Dreams are the touchstones of our character.
-Henry David Thoreau

Go confidently in the direction of your dreams.
Live the life you've imagined.
-Henry David Thoreau

"I will refresh the weary and satisfy the faint,"
says the Lord.
Jeremiah 31:25

Smile

Too often we underestimate the power of a touch,
a smile, a kind word, a listening ear,
an honest compliment, or the smallest act of caring:
all of which have the potential to turn a life around.
-Leo Buscaglia

"When the first baby laughed for the first time,
the laugh broke into thousands of pieces
and they all went skipping about,
and that was the beginning of fairies."
(from Peter Pan)

A smile is a whisper of a laugh.
-A child's definition

A happy heart makes the face cheerful.
Proverbs 15:13

Snow

Sunshine is delicious, rain is refreshing,
wind braces us up, snow is exhilarating;
there is really no such thing as bad weather,
only different kinds of good weather.
-John Ruskin

If peace be in the heart,
the wildest winter storm is full of solemn beauty.
-C. F. Richardson

A lot of people like snow.
I find it to be an unnecessary
freezing of water.
-Carl Reiner

Snowflakes falling,
Winter calling.
-Julie Perkins Cantrell

Son

(see also Baby, Boy and Child)

There is a harmony and beauty in the life of mother
and son that brims the mind's cup of satisfaction.
-Christopher Morley

The night you were born, I ceased being
my father's boy and became my son's father.
That night I began a new life.
-Henry Gregor Felson

A son can light up your day just
with a blink of his big, bright eyes.
-Crystal Dawn Perry

Sports
(see also specific sports)
Life's a ball when you're having fun.

Winners never quit and quitters never win.
-Vince Lombardi

*One man can be a crucial ingredient on a team,
but one man cannot make a team.*
-Kareem Abdul-Jabbar

You never really lose until you stop trying.
-Mike Ditka

*Think of yourself as an athlete.
I guarantee you it will change the way you stand,
the way you walk, and the decision
you make about your body.*
-Mariah Burton Nelson

Champions keep playing until they get it right.
-Billy Jean King

*Some plays just come out of me, just on instincts.
I'll make a play and wonder, How did I do that?*
-Roberto Alomar Baltimore

Spouse
*We have strange and wonderful relationship.
He's strange and I'm wonderful.*

*There is no more lovely, friendly,
and charming relationship, communion,
or company than a good marriage.*
-Martin Luther

Spring

If winter comes, can spring be far behind?
-Percy Shelley

Spring is nature's way of saying, "Let's party!"
-Robin Williams

*The day the Lord created hope
was probably the same day he created Spring.*
-Bern Williams

Star

*Baby's fishing for a dream, Fishing near and far,
His line a silver moonbeam, His bait a silver star.*
-Alice C.D. Riley

*Be glad of life because it gives you
the chance to love, and to work,
and to play and to look up at the stars.*
-Henry Van Dyke

Hitch your wagon to a star.
-Ralph Waldo Emerson

*You brighten my life through storm and rain
Like a million stars shining...forever*
-Najah T. Clemmons

There was a star danced, and under that was I born.
-William Shakespeare

*I will love the light for it shows me the way.
Yet I will endure the darkness
for it shows me the stars.*
-Og Mandino

St. Patrick's Day

May good luck be with you wherever you go, and your blessings outnumber the shamrocks that grow.

-Irish proverb

Style

Art produces ugly things which frequently become more beautiful with time. Fashion, on the other hand, produces beautiful things which always become ugly with time.

-Jean Cocteau

Beauty of style and harmony and grace and good rhythm depend on simplicity.

-Plato

Nineties style isn't.

-David Borenstein

Success

To be successful, the first thing to do is fall in love with your work.

-Sister Mary Lauretta

Go confidently in the direction of your dreams. Live the life you've imagined.

-Henry David Thoreau

That man is a success who has lived well, laughed often and loved much.

-Robert Louis Stevenson

Summer

Summer afternoon, summer afternoon...
to me, those have always been the two most
beautiful words in the English language.

-Henry James

Sunshine

Keep your face to the sunshine
and you cannot see the shadows.

-Helen Keller

Sunshine is delicious, rain is refreshing,
wind braces us up, snow is exhilarating;
there is really no such thing as bad weather,
only different kinds of good weather.

-John Ruskin

Sunshine on my shoulders makes me happy.

-John Denver

Love comforteth like sunshine after rain.

-William Shakespeare

There are painters who transform the sun to a
yellow spot, but there are others who
with the help of their art and their intelligence,
transform a yellow spot into sun.

-Pablo Picasso

She has the spirit of the sun,
The moods of the moon,
The will of the wind.

-Julie Perkins Cantrell

Our friendship brings sunshine to shade,
and shade to sunshine.
-Thomas Burke

So never let a cloudy day ruin your sunshine,
for even if you can't see it, the sunshine is still there,
inside of you ready to shine when you will let it.
-Amy Pitzele

Laughter is the sun
that drives winter from the human face.
-Victor Hugo

To love and to be loved
is to feel the sun from both sides.
-David Viscott

Swimming
Nobody can be in good health is he does not have
fresh air, sunshine, and good water.
-Unknown

Thousands have lived without love,
not one without water.
W.H. Auden

Talking
We spend the first twelve months of our children's lives
teaching them to walk and talk and the next twelve
telling them to sit down and shut up.
-Prochnow

A mother understands what a child does not say.
-Jewish proverb

Grant me the power of saying things
too simple and too sweet for words.
-Coventry Patmore

One of life's greatest pleasures is conversation.
-Sidney Smith

First you have to teach a child to talk,
then you have to teach it to be quiet.
-Prochnow

A word aptly spoken is like
apples of gold in settings of silver.
Proverbs 25:11

Out of the overflow of the heart the mouth speaks.
Matthew 12:34

Teacher
To teach is to learn twice.
-Joseph Joubert

What we learn with pleasure we never forget.
-Louis Mercier

For the mother is and must be,
whether she knows it or not, the greatest, strongest
and most lasting teacher her children have.
-Hannah Whitall Smith

Take in all that you have learned then
teach it in a way that has never been taught before.
-Vincent Ivan Phipps

Teenager

To our children, we give two things;
one is roots, the other wings.

The best way to keep children at home is to make the
home atmosphere pleasant
-and let the air out of their tires.

-Dorothy Parker

Human beings are the only creatures on
Earth that allow their children
to come back home.

-Bill Cosby

Be yourself! Who else is better qualified?

-Frank J. Giblin

You know your children are growing up
when they stop asking you where they
came from and refuse to tell you
where they're going.

-P.J. O'Rourke

What America needs is more young
people who will carry to their jobs the
same enthusiasm for getting ahead that
they display in traffic.

-Unknown

Never lend your car to anyone
to whom you have given birth.

-Erma Bombeck

If you obey all the rules you miss all the fun.

-Katharine Hepburn

The greatest discovery of any generation is
that human beings can alter their lives
by altering their attitudes.
-Albert Schweitzer

Life begins as a quest of the child for the man and
ends as a journey by the man to rediscover the child.
-Laurens van der Post

Thanksgiving

An open home, an open heart,
here grows a bountiful harvest.
-Judy Hand

Best of all, it is to preserve everything in a
pure, still heart, and let there be for every pulse
a thanksgiving, and for every breath a song.
-Konrad von Gesner

Who does not thank for little will not thank for much.
-Estonian proverb

Thanksgiving is a time of quiet reflection upon the past
and an annual reminder that God has, again, been
ever so faithful. The solid and simple things of life
are brought into clear focus.
-Charles R. Swindoll

Thank the Lord for his steadfast love,
for his wonderful works to humankind.
For he satisfies the thirsty,
and the hungry he fills with good things.
Psalm 107:8-9

From the fullness of his grace we have all received one blessing after another.

John 1:16

Everything God created is good, and nothing is to be rejected if it is received with thanksgiving.

1 Timothy 4:4

Toddler
(see also Baby and Child)

We spend the first twelve months of our children's lives teaching them to walk and talk and the next twelve telling them to sit down and shut up. First you have to teach a child to talk, then you have to teach it to be quiet.

-Prochnow

Toys

The child had every toy his father wanted.

-Robert E. Whitten

Travel
(see also Vacation)

To a friend's house, the road is never long.

The world is a book and those who do not travel read only one page.

-St. Augustine

So much of who we are is where we have been.

-William Langewiesche

Adventure is worthwhile.

-Amelia Earhart

*I have found out that there ain't no surer way to
find out whether you like people or hate them
than to travel with them.*
-Mark Twain

It's a very short trip. While alive, live.
-Malcom Forbes

A wise man travels to discover himself.
-James Russell Lowell

*Though we travel the world over to find the beautiful,
we must carry it with us, or we find it not.*
-Ralph Waldo Emerson

Trouble

*Expect trouble as an inevitable part of life and repeat
to yourself the most comforting words of all:
This too shall pass.*
-Ann Landers

If you obey all the rules you miss all the fun.
-Katherine Hepburn

*My mother had a great deal of trouble with me,
but I think she enjoyed it.*
-Mark Twain

*I believe in getting into hot water;
it keeps you clean.*
-G.K. Chesterton(1874 - 1936)

*Any child can tell you that the sole purpose of a
middle name is so he can tell when he's in trouble.*
-Dennis Fakes

I can resist anything but temptation.
-Oscar Wilde

Double, double toil and trouble.
-William Shakespeare

*If it were going to be easy to raise kids,
it wouldn't have started with something called labor.*
-Unknown

*If evolution really works,
how come mothers only have two hands?*
-Milton Berle

*A baby is always more trouble than you thought
-and more wonderful.*
-Charles Osgood

Turtle
*Behold the tortoise.
He makes progress only when he sticks his neck out.*
-James B. Conant

Twins
*There are two things in life for which we are never
fully prepared, and that is twins.*
-Josh Billings

Double, double toil and trouble.
-William Shakespeare

*It is not economical to go to bed early
to save the candles if the result is twins.*
-Chinese Proverb

All who would win joy must share it;
happiness was born a twin.

Lord Byron (1788 - 1824)

Persistence is the twin sister of excellence.
One is a matter of quality;
the other, a matter of time.

Marabel Morgan

Vacation
(see also Travel)

The rainy days that a man saves for,
usually seem to arrive during his vacation.

No man needs a vacation so much
as the man who has just had one.

-Elbert Hubbard

It isn't how much time you spend somewhere
that makes it memorable; it's how you spend the time.

-David Brenner

Volunteer

Hands to work, hearts to God.

-Shaker saying

We ourselves feel that what we are
doing is just a drop in the ocean
but the ocean would be less
because of that missing drop.

-Mother Teresa

Service is the rent that you pay for room on this earth.

-Shirley Chisholm

*Whoever renders service to many puts
himself in line for greatness
-great wealth, great return,
great satisfaction, great reputation, and great joy.*

-Jim Rohn

*The miracle is this-
the more we share, the more we have.*

-Leonard Nimoy

*It is one of the most beautiful compensations
of this life that you cannot sincerely try to
help another without helping yourself.*

-Ralph Waldo Emerson

*All labor that uplifts humanity has dignity and
importance and should be undertaken
with painstaking excellence.*

-Martin Luther King, Jr.

*The highest reward for a man's toil is
not what he gets for it but what he becomes by it.*

-John Ruskin

*Each one should use whatever gift he has received
to serve others, faithfully administering
God's grace in various forms.*

1 Peter 4:10

Walking

Every little step gets us closer to where we're going.

The journey of one thousand miles
must begin with a single step.
-Chinese Proverb

Fall seven times, stand up eight.
-Japanese proverb

The distance is nothing.
It's only the first step that's important.
-Marquise Du Deffand

If you are seeking creative ideas, go out walking.
Angels whisper to a man when he goes for a walk.
-Raymond Inman

By perseverance the snail reached the ark.
-Charles Haddon Spurgeon

We spend the first twelve months of our children's lives
teaching them to walk and talk and the next twelve
telling them to sit down and shut up.
-Prochnow

If you can walk, you can dance.
-Zimbabwe saying

Many people will walk in and out of your life
but only a true friend will leave footprints in your heart.
-Eleanor Roosevelt

Wedding
(see also Love)

To have and to hold from this day forward...
two souls but with a single thought
-two hearts that beat as one.

-Maria Lovell

There is no more lovely,
Friendly and charming relationship,
Communion or company
Than a good marriage.

-Martin Luther

What therefore God hath joined together,
let not man put asunder.

Mark 10:9

Windows

Children are like windows that open
onto the future as well as the past,
the external world as well as
our own private landscapes.

-Jane Swigart

Let there be many windows to your soul,
that all the glory of the world
may beautify it.

-Ella Wheeler Wilcox

Winter

If winter comes, can spring be far behind?

-Percy Shelley

Laughter is the sun
that drives winter from the human face.

-Victor Hugo

Work

You can grow up to be anything you want to be.

Don't make a living at the expense of life.

To be successful,
the first thing to do is fall in love with your work.
-Sister Mary Lauretta

Choose a job you love,
and you will never have to work a day in your life.
-Confucius

The work will wait while you show the child the rainbow;
but the rainbow won't wait while you do the work.
-Patricia Clafford

All labor that uplifts humanity has dignity
and importance and should be undertaken
with painstaking excellence.
-Martin Luther King, Jr.

The supreme accomplishment is to blur the line
between work and play.
-Arnold Toynbee

Work is what you do so that some time
you won't have to do it anymore.
-Alfred Polgar

What America needs is more young people
who will carry to their jobs the same
enthusiasm for getting ahead
that they display in traffic.
-Unknown

Hands to work, hearts to God.
-Shaker saying

Honest labor bears a lovely face.
-Thomas Dekker

*Be glad of life because it gives you
the chance to love, and to work,
and to play and to look up at the stars.*
-Henry Van Dyke

*Work has to include our deepest values and
passions and feelings and commitments,
or it's not work, it's just a job.*
-Matthew Fox

Do what you love, the money will follow.
-Marsha Sinetar

Diligent hands bring wealth.
Proverbs 10:4

Wrestling
(see also Sports)
*You can either stand up and be counted
or lie down and be counted out.*

Quotes:

Quotes:

Quotes:

Quotes:

www.clearskypublishing.com

Sweet Impressions by Dana

Dana Clark's love of writing inspired her to create her own greeting card line, Sweet Impressions by Dana. In addition to her pre-printed cards, she can personalize a special poem for you, saying just what you feel, for a birthday, wedding, any special occasion, or just to say, "I love you."

Dana Roberts Clark
Sweet Impressions by Dana
(706) 935-6841

*A word of thanks to God, my Father, for the talents he has given me, to Chris, my husband, for putting up with all my crazy dreams and to Grace, Faith, and Hope, my inspirations.
Enjoy the poetry,
Dana R. Clark

A.R.T. Cards, etc.
It's Your Party

Artist, writer and poet, Laura Taylor Mark creates original artwork, poetry and gifts for her company, A.R.T. Cards, etc. Her love of collage, watercolor painting and textural elements is reflected in her whimsical, one-of-a-kind paper art. For custom work, the gift giver and recipient are always kept in mind during the creative process. The result is a truly unique and memorable keepsake of a special occasion or event.

Laura Taylor Mark, Artist/Writer/Poet
Studio #: (906) 635-0084

Laura's A.R.T Cards, etc.
www.artcardsetc.com

It's Your Party
Party & Event Planning Service
www.itsyourpartybiz.com

Are you looking at a friend's book?
If you would like your own copy,
please check with your
local scrapbook store or visit us at:

www.clearskypublishing.com

Check out our other great products too!